AN ARCHITECTURAL ALBUM: CHICAGO'S NORTH SHORE

JUNIOR LEAGUE OF EVANSTON, INC.
EVANSTON, ILLINOIS

AN ARCHITECTURAL ALBUM: CHICAGO'S NORTH SHORE

THE JUNIOR LEAGUE OF EVANSTON, INC.

BELINDA S. BLANCHARD
Project Director

SUSAN S. BENJAMIN
Architectural Historian & Editor

DAVID CLIFTON
Photographer

SUZANNE THOMAS
Copy Editor

ELLEN KETTLER PASELTINER
Appendix Contributor

OLVER DUNLOP ASSOCIATES INC.
Graphic Design

With text by:
Susan S. Benjamin
Belinda S. Blanchard
Kathleen S. Cassidy
Kirby Lewis Colson
Diane G. Drinker
Claudia S. Lane
Ellen Kettler Paseltiner
Betsy S. Ryberg
Caren M. Wolf

Published by the Junior League of Evanston, Inc.

The Junior League of Evanston, Inc.
reaches out to all young women regardless
of race, religion, color, or national origin
who demonstrate an interest in
and a commitment to voluntarism.

First Printing 1988

Set in Goudy Oldstyle, printed on Eloquence paper
Printed and bound in the United States by
Mossberg & Co. Inc.

Library of Congress Catalog Card Number 88-082-693

Dedicated to all volunteers committed to promoting voluntarism
and to improving the community through the effective action
and leadership of trained volunteers.

The Junior League of Evanston, Inc.

The proceeds of this book support the projects and programs
of the Junior League of Evanston, Inc.

TABLE OF CONTENTS

An Analogous Album

Flattered as I am to be invited to write a foreword to the domestic meanderings of Chicago's North Shore architects and their clients throughout this past century, one's appetite is whetted even more by the prospect of perusing this album not as a picture portrait describing the way we were, but rather as a clue to what it is we might become. The concept of explaining something by comparing it point by point with something else fascinates me almost as much as the potential that certain admitted resemblances imply probable further similarity.

What immediately comes to mind is Leonard Eaton's brilliant comparison of those two creative forces at the turn of the century — Howard van Doren Shaw and Frank Lloyd Wright — and for that matter, a comparison of their clients as well. American suburbs continue to beckon to families of disparate economic capabilities outlined by Professor Eaton — the new, as well as the old, rich. Connoisseurship — or simply, taste (good and godawful) — continues to dominate the ways in which these clients and their architects go about the business of an architectural

production that exploits antecedents by way of legitimating the very presence of the families hidden behind the walls of the dwellings seen herein.

The preponderance of architecture informed if not by nostalgia, then at least by reference (or quotation), dominates the pages that follow. While there are rare examples of what might be construed as avant-gardism in forming the architecture of the American suburb (Frank Lloyd Wright, George Fred Keck, Henry Dubin, David Haid), the vast majority of the architectural information here presented is "historicist" in nature. Not necessarily influenced by Classical architecture alone, this work is also informed by the tradition nostalgically referred to as "vernacular" (a western influence that is thought to emanate from the British "Keep" of the Middle Ages).

The Classical influence is here represented by such architects as: Philip Maher, Daniel Burnham, David Adler, Shepley, Rutan and Coolidge, Arthur Heun, and Hammond, Beeby and Babka. The Vernacular influence is adequately exemplified by: Howard van Doren Shaw, George Maher, Tallmadge and Watson, Henry Ives Cobb, Henry Edwards Ficken and Charles Frost. Both the Classical as well as the Vernacular traditions are referential, and as such, are deferential. By referring to earlier models of gentrification, they defer to those traditions as well.

The continuing presence of both traditions implies an ever expanding loss of faith in a present that can only be construed to be absent. A continuation of both traditions seems inferred by the increasing number of domestic variations on each of those themes. Clearly, the American suburb is informed by nostalgic desires of a return to deeply sought after origins not apparently possible in the architecture of the day. It may be that the American city is a more promising venue for architectural experimentation than is the American suburb. After all, the suburb is the "escape" from the density of metropolitan life referred to by such artists at the turn of the century as Edward Munch and George Ensor.

Apparently, nostalgia is best pursued in the privacy of nature rather than in the naked spotlight of the city, and if nothing else, this work is a study into the permutations of nostalgically derived architectural forms as a response, I would submit, to the pressures of city life and its corresponding density. The photographs in this analogous album bear witness to the ideality of suburban life grown to an age where nature has, through time, been allowed to regain its forest-like furtiveness, and where man-made built form has receded into a kind of Edenic situation.

Given the power of precedent, it is likely that other analogous albums in other analogous epochs will present themselves much in the same spirit as this one where the hybridization common to American architecture will continue to inform the domestic urges of other analogous families as they seek, each in their turn, to return to the absent original for which they desperately yearn. But in that search, there may be others who question the absence of presence, just as I have attempted to do, hoping that a future will look forward through the vehicle of its experiments, even as it looks backwards for verification to its ancestral roots.

Stanley Tigerman
Chicago, August 1988

ACKNOWLEDGMENTS

The scope of "An Architectural Album: Chicago's North Shore" was enormous. Inspired by the Junior League of Lincoln's book, "An Architectural Album of Lincoln, Nebraska," the Junior League of Evanston, Inc. (JLE) began what would be a four year project. Beginning in 1984 with the knowledge that no other book exactly like this existed and the firm conviction that it should and could be done, the process began with the full support of the voting membership. The mission of the project was to educate the public on the significant architecture found in the communities of the North Shore of Chicago with the hope that through education there would be protection for these buildings. The task was very challenging as the committee members began a survey of buildings throughout the North Shore. After compiling an initial roster of hundreds of buildings, the committee narrowed the list to the ninety entries here. This was the work of many Junior League and community volunteers named at the end of the book.

Initial thanks go to the original committee who spent two years researching the entries in each community using resources from local governments, historical societies, libraries, museums and preservation commissions. Much gratitude is due the staffs of the many organizations that were supportive and helped supply the information needed.

Personal thanks are given to Susan Benjamin, architectural historian, for her expertise and dedication and to David Clifton, architectural photographer, for his cooperation and talent.

The completion of the project acknowledges the JLE Board of Directors, Executive Committee, Community Council, Finance Council, Marketing Committee, the Historic Preservation and the Arts Focus Area, and Thrift House (JLE's financial base), without which a large project like this could not have been undertaken.

Two JLE members, Beth Mikel and Bonnie Winn, deserve special thanks for their unselfish devotion to the completion of the project.

Pivotal to the project are the building owners who graciously shared their houses or buildings and helped so much with the actual research.

One last word of thanks, for their patience and support, to the families of the volunteers who made "An Architectural Album: Chicago's North Shore" a reality.

Suzie (Belinda S.) Blanchard

INTRODUCTION

Chicago's North Shore is an architectural treasure trove. Miles of tree-lined streets exhibit the very best examples of architectural styles from Victorian through Post Modern. Since the mid-1800s the chain of nine suburbs —Evanston to Lake Bluff—along the western shore of Lake Michigan, commonly referred to as the North Shore, offered increasingly affluent city-weary Chicagoans opportunity to live in their own (often architect-designed) home on a spacious lot.

The American dream was first realized on the North Shore with construction of Victorian Gothic and Italianate houses popularized by Andrew Jackson Downing. Downing could be called a suburban evangelist, for he preached the virtues of the villa in a pastoral setting as the ideal environ for American domesticity. The romantic yearning for time past was translated in the 1870s and 1880s into stately family homes with wide porches, projecting bays and tall towers, all painted in rich colors to accentuate ornamental detailing. Builders of these early homes were typically carpenters and cabinet makers who could convert Downing's pattern book designs into

reality. The North Shore's sylvan setting, with deep glacier-cut ravines, provided expansive surroundings for the Victorian house and inspiration for Hotchkiss in Lake Forest (1858) and Horace W.S. Cleveland and William French in Highland Park (1868) to lay out towns with winding streets in keeping with the natural topography.

At the turn of the century, architecture began to change. "Revival" was the key word in building design, but the resulting work was not the romantic's interpretation; it was a literal translation of past styles. America's British and Eastern seaboard roots were carefully studied. Architects, many of whom had traditional training at the Massachusetts Institute of Technology or the École des Beaux Arts, became historians, familiarizing themselves with architecture's Classical, as well as recent, past. More and more trained professionals set up practice in Chicago, attracting clients who had increasing amounts of disposable income. Chicagoans' attitudes were being strongly influenced by more extensive travel and visits to the 1893 World's Columbian Exposition.

It is only natural for the increasingly worldly North Shore residents to have looked to their roots for inspiration

when they wanted comfort and respectability in their homes. The Colonial Revival style became the most popular. Second was Tudor Revival. Whether inspired by the Cotswold cottage or the English Manor house, there evolved what has been described as an "Anglomania" that permeated commercial and residential architecture. Examples of other Revival styles, although fewer in number, add diversity to the North Shore's architectural fabric.

At the same time that historical revivalism was becoming more popular, shortly before 1900, Frank Lloyd Wright and his followers were developing America's first indigenous modern residential style. Taking inspiration from the Midwest's most persistent natural feature, the prairie, Wright created brilliant geometric compositions, emphatically horizontal, unlike anything that preceded them. Fine Prairie School buildings by Wright and his followers, George Maher, Thomas Tallmadge, Vernon Watson, Louis Guenzel, William Drummond and John Van Bergen, are found throughout the North Shore.

The heritage of recent modern architecture also is well represented.

George Fred Keck and William Keck were in the forefront of experimentation in passive solar architecture and designed subdivisions as well as several award-winning custom homes. Mies van der Rohe's disciples and International Style architects never had a profound impact, but there are excellent examples on the North Shore. The most avant garde Post Modern architecture is illustrated by the work of Stanley Tigerman and Thomas Beeby.

With the help of Chicago architects, many of whom lived in these communities, North Shore residents settled in an environment that married city and rural life, yet was different from both. The suburbanite didn't desire to be a farmer or a hermit in the wilderness but simply wanted to put some distance between work and home life.

From early on, the attraction of the North Shore was its park-like atmosphere and hilly terrain. Many Chicagoans first spent summers on the North Shore and, captivated by the environment, stayed, building homes that reflect in their design quality the sheer beauty of the surroundings. Landscape architects were inspired. Jens Jensen, who lived in Wilmette and had an office in Highland Park, used native plant material to create placid retreats; others designed manicured landscapes to create a more formal environment.

There were several reasons that Chicagoans wished to move from the city's core. As Chicago was becoming increasingly industrialized, those who prospered no longer wanted to live and raise families near their companies. This wish partially grew out of a general distrust for the large immigrant population, stemming from labor unrest in the 1880s; a disgust with political corruption; a fear of crime; and a well-founded terror of fire that lingered after the Great Chicago Fire of 1871. Devastating one-third of the city, the fire destroyed 17,450 buildings, took 250 lives and left 98,000 people homeless. Chicago was becoming noisy, dirty and congested. In 1870, the city's population was 298,977; by 1900, it was 1.7 million and by 1920 it was 2.7 million.

The Chicago & North Western Railway provided the means for escape from Chicago's problems to a more idyllic setting. The trains were com-fortable, prompt, clean and reasonable. As early as 1873 there were 11 trains running between Chicago and the North Shore suburbs. There was rush hour express service — even private subscription cars.

Not much has changed over the years. The trains run on time; the landscape is respected and the architecture is admired. Many conscientious residents are restoring their homes. Several of the communities have passed landmark ordinances. Owners of National Register properties point to them with pride.

The North Shore has set an excellent precedent for itself and others, illustrating what a suburban area can become. With a persistent commitment to preserving its unique architectural heritage in order to establish a standard for future development, North Shore architecture will remain the embodiment of the American dream.

Susan Sinykin Benjamin

Francis E. Willard House
Rest Cottage
1730 Chicago Avenue
Evanston, Illinois

Rest Cottage, built in 1865 with an 1878 addition, is a premiere example of Carpenter Gothic architecture on Chicago's North Shore. Vertical board and batten siding, steep gabled roofs with crisply-cut ornamental bargeboard, also called gingerbread, and finials emphasize the vertical design and loosely relate the building to Europe's great Gothic cathedrals. The relationship is more sentimental than literal. With stone expensive and scarce and skilled stone masons generally unavailable, these homes were modest, built of wood by local carpenters, hence the stylistic name Carpenter Gothic. Sometimes they are known as Victorian Gothic.

Beyond its stylistic excellence, Rest Cottage is noteworthy as the home of Frances E. Willard, an acknowledged leader in women's education, suffrage and the temperance movement. At age 32, she became president of the Evanston College for Ladies. When the college was absorbed by Northwestern University in 1873, she was made dean of women. Her real fame, however, came as a leader of the temperance movement, serving as national president of the Women's Christian Temperance Union (WCTU) in 1879 and founder of the world organization in 1891. Miss Willard spent her time speaking and traveling for the cause until her death in 1898.

The house is a National Historic Landmark. It is largely furnished with Miss Willard's personal belongings and is maintained as a public museum by the WCTU.

Private Residence
701 Forest Avenue
Evanston, Illinois

A Victorian home, to be "proper," had to wear historic dress. This Italianate house, built in 1872, is typical. In design, it is derived from an Italian villa. Like all Victorians built in the 1860s and 1870s, the house is not a literal imitation of a past style. Rather, it is a romantic vision of a Tuscan villa, complete with tower, intended to evoke the beauty of the Italian countryside.

The Italianate style was popularized by American pattern books, especially those written by Andrew Jackson Downing in the 1840s and 1850s. Homeowners and local builders could simply follow the plans. Italianates and Victorian Gothics in the Midwest were generally not architect-designed and tended to be smaller and less elaborate than their East Coast counterparts.

The house has several features characteristic of the Italianate style. Many had towers that have since been removed; it is the only Italianate in Evanston with its tower intact. The overall shape is irregular, reflecting an informal floor plan inside. The house is two stories, culminating in a broad hipped roof. The roof's deep cornice is supported by paired ornamental brackets, connected by a row of tooth-like dentils. Especially attractive is the tall, narrow triple window in the third floor tower. Deep hoodmolds, intended to deflect rainwater, top the rest of the windows. This is one of the finest Italianate houses on the North Shore.

Gross Point Lighthouse

2535 Sheridan Road
Evanston, Illinois

Completed in 1873, this 90-foot lighthouse was originally constructed of brick with a steel framed light at the top. By 1914, the brick walls had eroded and were sheathed with a 3½ inch protective layer of concrete. Today the structure stands as a tall, tapered column culminating in a circular walkway supported by carved brackets. Similar brackets support the cornice of the gatekeeper's cottage; they are like those typically found at the roofline of Italianate houses.

Several shipping disasters, including the collision of the paddlewheeler, Lady Elgin, with the lumber schooner, Augustus, in 1860, demonstrated the need for a lighthouse at this location, known as Gross Point. Petitioned by Evanston residents, Congress allocated $35,000 to build the lighthouse and keeper's quarters. They were designed by Major O.M. Poe of the U.S. Army. Although construction was delayed by the Civil War, the lighthouse became operational in 1874. The light continues to aid small craft.

Flanking the lighthouse are two small gable-roofed structures that originally were constructed in 1880 to house steam-powered fog sirens. The fog horns were removed in 1922, but the houses remain.

The Gross Point Lighthouse was listed on the National Register of Historic Places in 1976 and is open to the public. It was restored in the early 1980s.

Simeon Farwell House
1433 Hinman Avenue
Evanston, Illinois

John Mills Van Osdel, Chicago's first architect, designed 1433 Hinman in 1890. It is representative of the Queen Anne style that is fairly prevalent on the North Shore, especially near the older central parts of town.

Born in 1811, Van Osdel began his career in 1837, the year Chicago was incorporated, with a mansion for William B. Ogden, the city's first mayor. His career was prolific, and by his death in 1891 he had designed more than 73 commercial and public buildings in Chicago's Loop and many residences outside the city's central business area. To his credit are Chicago's City Hall and Market (1848); University Hall, the University of Chicago's first building (1859); and the first and second Palmer House hotels (1856, 1871). Unfortunately, all have been demolished, and there is little left of Van Osdel's commercial work.

The Queen Anne idiom that Van Osdel used in the Farwell House is an architectural style, popular in the 1880s and 1890s, characterized by a variety of contrasting shapes and surface textures. Steeply-pitched intersecting gable roofs, broad porches, round or polygonal corner towers and projecting bay windows typically combine to form a composition with considerable visual interest. Van Osdel's design ingenuity is particularly evident in the way he integrates his own brand of Sullivanesque ornamentation into the building's complicated array of roof shapes, window treatments and building materials.

The name of the style is curiously inappropriate and misleading, generally unrelated to the reign of Queen Anne (1702-1714) and the formal Renaissance architecture of that time.

Charles Jernegan House
1144 Michigan Avenue
Evanston, Illinois

Built in 1890, this house is one of the best examples of Shingle style architecture on the North Shore. Like the Queen Anne style from which it was derived, Shingle style buildings are irregular in shape and complicated in roof massing. A flared stone base that hugs the ground and a broad open porch are topped by the style's most characteristic feature, shingles that flow around the entire surface of the house like a thin skin. Windows barely seem to project. Of note is the curving eyebrow dormer. The tower, with its bell-shaped roof, is integrated into the building's shingled surface. Emphasis everywhere is on the graceful, rounded contours made possible by shingles. Unlike the 19th Century architectural styles that preceded it, including the Victorian Gothic, Italianate and Queen Anne, there is little ornamental detail. Shingle style buildings draw attention to the whole not the parts.

The style was born in New England, influenced by the American Colonial architecture prevalent in seaside towns like Newport, Rhode Island; Marblehead, Massachusetts; and Portsmouth, New Hampshire. The gambrel roof, a Dutch Colonial feature, was rediscovered and is often seen in Shingle style buildings. As Newport and the other towns became fashionable summering spots in the late 19th Century, many Shingle style houses were built. It is generally thought of as a suburban or resort style. There are some excellent examples on the North Shore, but the style never drew as much interest as the Queen Anne.

The house was built for Charles Jernegan, a member of the Chicago Board of Trade. Its designer, Enoch Hill Turnoch, once worked for William LeBaron Jenney, known as father of the skyscraper.

Charles Gates Dawes House
225 East Greenwood Street
Evanston, Illinois

The lavish Chateauesque mansion, home of the Charles Gates Dawes family for 48 years, is a furnished house museum run by the Evanston Historical Society. There is no better example of this unusual monumental style preserved on the North Shore.

The Chateauesque style, popular in the 1880s and 1890s, is derived from the large 16th Century chateaux built in France during the reign of Francois I. Masonry construction, massive towers, steep roofs and elaborate detailing inside and out characterize a style suitable only for the wealthiest of clients. This magnificent 28-room example was built in 1894 by prominent New York architect Henry Edwards-Ficken for Robert D. Sheppard, treasurer and business manager for Northwestern University. But it is associated primarily with long-time resident Charles Gates Dawes.

Dawes was born in 1865 in Marietta, Ohio. Well-known as a politician, author and philanthropist, he served as vice president under Calvin Coolidge, received the Nobel Peace Prize in 1925 for the Post World War I Dawes Plan for economic recovery of Europe and was ambassador to Great Britain between 1929 and 1932.

Recognizing the significance of his very special house, Dawes deeded it to Northwestern University, which leases it to the Evanston Historical Society. It has been home to the Society and the Junior League of Evanston since 1960. A designated National Historic Landmark, the Dawes house is open to the public.

John C. Linthicum House
1315 Forest Avenue
Evanston, Illinois

The John C. Linthicum house, designed in 1907 by the firm of Tallmadge and Watson, represents an intriguing blend of the bungalow with the Prairie School.

The bungalow, as it has come to be known, is a small, one-story house capped by a gable roof with a broad porch across the front. The style is prolific in Chicago and scattered throughout the North Shore. Derived from a mutation of the Hindu word "Bangla," meaning "belonging to Bengal," the word bungalow was used by the British in the early 1900s to describe resthouses built by the Indian government. A "dak-bungalow" was a temporary dwelling with a front veranda facing the road, a place for weary travelers.

Bungalows were built all over America between 1900-1920, taking many forms. In California, there are craftsman bungalows; in New England there are seacoast bungalows and in Chicago there are Prairie bungalows.

The Linthicum house is a large, elegant Prairie bungalow. It is related to the bungalow by its simplicity and wide front porch. But this is where the stylistic association ends. The design is more sophisticated; the house is distinctly Prairie School in its subtle crisp brickwork, horizontal massing, broad overhangs and beautiful stained glass windows. Much like work of George Maher, it has a long open porch, symmetrical massing and segmental arches.

Thomas Eddy Tallmadge, an Evanston resident, and Vernon S. Watson were the architects. The firm designed many North Shore houses, particularly in Evanston. They formed their own practice in 1905 with Watson as designer. Tallmadge is better known as a historian and writer, responsible for having coined the term "Chicago School" in 1908.

The Linthicum House is in the National Register Evanston Lake Shore Historic District.

Frederick B. Carter Jr. House
1024 Judson Avenue
Evanston, Illinois

The Frederick B. Carter Jr. house, designed in 1910, reflects the best work of architect Walter Burley Griffin. It was listed on the National Register of Historic Places in 1974. In this house, clearly derived from the architectural style of Frank Lloyd Wright, Griffin utilizes Prairie School elements in a sophisticated, personal way. Its ribbon windows, interlocking geometric shapes and broad overhangs make the house Prairie; its angularity, simplified windows with wood muntins and combined use of brick and stucco make it Griffin.

Walter Burley Griffin was born in 1876 and raised in Oak Park where Wright built his own house in 1889 and established his practice. Graduating from the University of Illinois in 1899, Griffin immediately took loft space at Steinway Hall (demolished). Here he shared ideas and a communal drafting space with other young architects including Wright, Allen and Irving Pond, Myron Hunt, Robert C. Spencer Jr. and Dwight Perkins. Between 1902 and 1906, when he established his own practice, he worked as a draftsman for Wright in the Oak Park studio. It is clear why Griffin's Prairie School work is generally unblemished by other stylistic influences.

Equally well-known is Griffin's wife, Marion Mahoney Griffin, whom he met when they were working in Wright's studio. Marion Mahoney was one of the first women graduates of Massachusetts Institute of Technology (1894), but is remembered for her exquisite renderings of Wright's work. She worked for Wright from 1895 until 1911, when she married Griffin and their careers merged, taking a turn toward community planning. In 1911, he won the competition to design Canberra's new capital, and they moved to Australia.

Edward Kirk Warren House
2829 Sheridan Place
Evanston, Illinois

Numerous examples of Tudor Revival architecture are found throughout the North Shore. Some, like the Edward Kirk Warren house, designed in 1910 by William Carbys Zimmerman, are large and stately, based on the English manor house. Americans seeking respectability reached further than their Colonial roots to Great Britain for a proper antecedent. Tudor Revival became popular around 1910 and flourished in the 1920s as more and more upper middle class residents made the North Shore their home.

Tudor elements abound in the Warren house. It is asymmetrical with a steeply-pitched front gable rising above the roofline. Leaded casement windows divided into rectangular sections by stone mullions are capped by moldings shaped into flat Tudor arches. The roof is slate. An octagonal medieval tower with battlements at the top houses a staircase to the left of the entrance. Five grotesques, mythical beasts, support the cornice of the tower. The house differs from other North Shore Tudors, large and small, in its use of smooth-surfaced stone rather than the typical brick with stone trim. The effect is elegant and imposing.

Zimmerman was engaged to design a 15-room house and an adjacent 5-room garage. Although not well-known, Zimmerman studied at Massachusetts Institute of Technology, worked in the office of Daniel Burnham and designed several large homes for prominent families in Chicago, Evanston and Lake Forest. Ironically, he seems to be best remembered as the architect of the Illinois State Penitentiary at Joliet. He was Illinois State Architect between 1905 and 1913.

Zimmerman's client for this house, Edward Kirk Warren, was a businessman from Three Oaks, Michigan. When he moved into his new Evanston home in 1912 at age 63, he named it Three Oaks. It is listed on the National Register of Historic Places.

George B. Dryden House
1314 Ridge Avenue
Evanston, Illinois

Architect George Maher is typically associated with the Prairie School movement yet this textbook Georgian, which he designed in 1916, clearly illustrates his design versatility. In this house Maher considered the wishes of his client, industrialist George B. Dryden, and modelled Dryden's house after the 1905 Georgian Revival house of his wife's uncle, George Eastman.

The dignity, monumentality and Classical inspiration of Georgian Revival architecture is reflected in even a small section of the 30-room Dryden mansion. It is a three-story red brick structure with an imposing two-story pedimented entrance portico. Classical details abound: stone columns with Corinthian capitals, rounded pilasters supporting molded cornices, brick quoining, modillions and dentils. Maher carefully reproduced a Georgian Revival house, setting it on a 2½ acre site with a generous front lawn facing Ridge Avenue, one of Evanston's most distinguished streets.

George B. Dryden was born in Ohio in 1869. In 1901 he married the niece and heiress of George Eastman of Rochester, New York. "Uncle George" was the founder of the Eastman Kodak Company. Dryden, distinguishing himself, founded the Dryden Rubber Company. Active in community affairs, he served on several boards including Northwestern University and Evanston Hospital.

Architect George Washington Maher is best known for his bold individualistic Prairie School residential designs, many of which are located on the North Shore. Less well-known as a preservationist, he played a pivotal role in the restoration and recycling of Charles B. Atwood's Fine Arts Building after the World's Columbian Exposition of 1893. It now serves as the Museum of Science and Industry.

Maher's George Dryden house is listed on the National Register of Historic Places. It currently serves as Evanston School District 65 offices.

33

The Lake Shore Apartments
470-498 Sheridan Road
Evanston, Illinois

The North Shore suburbs are frequently associated with single family homes on large well-landscaped lots. Only in Evanston is there a concentration of apartment buildings. Built roughly between 1900 and 1930, they fit their suburban setting. Most are brick, three stories over an English basement, embellished with handsome ornamentation, light and airy on the interior and built to surround a spacious, landscaped lawn or court. These courtyard apartments were designed specifically to appeal to a "better class" clientele and to have all the comforts of home: fireplaces, elegant stylistic detailing, built-ins and sun porches with views onto the court.

Many Evanston apartments have maids' rooms, internal vacuum systems, private garages, even safes. None are as opulent as New York apartments or as grand in size as many Chicago apartments on Lake Shore Drive. Rather, they are simple and elegant, suited to the North Shore.

This building epitomizes the best of the suburban apartment type. Built in 1927, it has 42 four- to six-room units facing Lake Michigan or a handsome private courtyard entered through a brick and terra-cotta arcade. The apartments on the third floor have 15-foot ceilings. Stylistically, the building is Georgian with Classical details — pediments, swags and urns. It was designed by Roy T. France who specialized in apartment buildings and apartment hotels.

Advertised in a 1928 real estate publication, "Portfolio of Fine Apartment Homes," the Lake Shore was touted as "thoroughly modern." The apartments were praised for their large rooms, scientifically planned kitchens with butlers' pantries, incinerators and porcelain appliances and "the remarkable absence of corridors." Even with an inside garage for 35 automobiles, limousine transportation was provided to the "L," train and schools.

The Lake Shore is one of 49 Evanston apartment buildings listed on the National Register of Historic Places under the theme "Suburban Apartment Buildings in Evanston, Illinois."

Marshall Field & Company Building
1700 Sherman Avenue
Evanston, Illinois

The store designed for Marshall Field & Company in 1929 is unlike any commercial structure on the North Shore. It was designed to stand alone, not to fit into the surrounding architectural fabric. Built as one of the first suburban branches of Chicago's pre-eminent department store, its sophisticated design is clearly meant to reflect the store's desired image. The building's twin is in Oak Park.

In the business districts of North Shore towns the best architecture is generally Tudor and fits together to form a small-scale cozy, English village. This is best typified by Howard Van Doren Shaw's Market Square in Lake Forest. The Field building is different. Here is an imposing five-story building capped by a mansard roof. There are large first-floor display windows surrounded by elegant abstract geometric Art Deco trim.

Today mansard roofs tend to be used on buildings that are two or three stories; the overall effect is that of a lady whose hat is too big. They were originally intended for tall structures. The first known use was in the 17th Century by Francois Mansart in the Louvre. The mansard roof was exploited during the reign of Napoleon III in the 19th Century to get around Paris building height limits. It was a clever way of adding a whole floor of rentable space, carefully tucked under a building's roof.

Graham, Anderson, Probst and White, a large, noteworthy Chicago firm, designed the building. It was the successor firm to Daniel H. Burnham's. When Burnham died in 1912, Ernest K. Graham, who was Burnham's construction superintendent at the 1893 World's Columbian Exposition, assumed leadership of his office, then established his own firm. Graham, Anderson, Probst and White, whose work was diverse and prolific, designed many of Chicago's finest buildings. These include the Field Museum (1911-1919), the Wrigley Building (1919-1923), the Shedd Aquarium (1929), the Civic Opera Building (1929) and the Merchandise Mart (1930).

Bahai Temple
100 Linden Street
Wilmette, Illinois

Wilmette's spectacular Bahai Temple is one of seven in the world. The second to be constructed, it was funded totally by voluntary contributions from the world's Bahai community. Originating in Persia, the Bahai faith encompasses all religions. It promotes universal peace, equality of the sexes and races, compulsory education and a common international language. The Bahai religion was introduced to the Chicago area by a missionary who came to the World's Columbian Exposition in 1893.

The ground breaking ceremony for the Bahai Temple and dedication address by 'Abdu'l Baha, son of Bah'a'u'llah, Bahai founder and world leader, took place in 1912. French Canadian architect Louis Bourgeois was the building's designer. Selected from a public competition, he took more than eight years to design this place of worship that expresses the universality of the Bahai religion. Its delicate lace-like ornamentation incorporates symbols from all the world's religions.

Bourgeois' design is executed in concrete made of crystalline quartz, opalescent quartz, sand and portland cement. This mix gives the structure a luminescent glow. Resting on nine caissons, dipping 124 feet to bedrock, the nine-sided Bahai Temple with a bell-shaped dome soars to 137 feet. The interior sanctuary is flooded with light, therefore its name: the Temple of Light. Above each of the nine sanctuary entrances are carved quotations from the Bahai writings.

The temple has a commanding presence, set high on its 6.97 acre artistically landscaped site overlooking Lake Michigan. Interestingly, the original temple design was twice its constructed size.

The Bahai Temple and grounds, which were not totally completed until 1952, is a National Historic Landmark.

Benjamin Hill House
219 Sixth Street
Wilmette, Illinois

The design for the Benjamin Hill house, built as a farmhouse in the Victorian Vernacular style, was probably taken from a pattern book. Containing simplified versions of the "latest" in Victorian houses, these books circulated widely throughout the United States. Details could be easily interpreted by local craftsmen because of 19th Century inventions. The elaborate gingerbread trim acknowledges the introduction of the steam-powered scroll saw. Carpenters could cut graceful and fanciful designs more quickly and economically than by hand.

Pediment-crowned hoodmolds over the windows and decorative brackets on the porch columns are typical design elements that lend this house the charm often associated with Victorian architecture. Others include etched glass, the large L-shaped porch and projecting bay window.

Reportedly, developer Benjamin Franklin Hill constructed this and other houses in the 1860s. He developed the southeast area of Wilmette, naming it "Hillsville" in honor of his father Aruna Hill, who settled in Wilmette in 1837. Benjamin Hill also owned much of the land near the railroad depot.

Vernacular cottages of the 19th Century are found scattered throughout the North Shore, remnants of the area's rural past. They are of local brick or sheathed in clapboard. Design elements are simple and sparse but often beautiful. Buildings such as the Hill house, once common, are becoming increasingly scarce.

Gross Point Village Hall
609 Ridge Road
Wilmette, Illinois

The Gross Point Village Hall symbolizes the hopes and dreams of farmers who left Germany starting in the 1840s to escape religious oppression.

Originally Gross Point stretched from Montrose Avenue and Graceland Cemetery (Chicago) to County Line Road in Highland Park. The village of Gross Point was incorporated March 10, 1874. Its Village Hall was built in 1896.

The Village Hall is representative of late 19th Century municipal buildings. It is tall and imposing, typical of Victorian design. Yet it is distinctive and noteworthy for precision brickwork. The crisp detailing speaks of the building's Germanic heritage. Dentils, moldings, pilasters and linear stone banding are highly simplified.

Designed by architect Alb. Fischer and built by Gross Point general contractor and tavern owner, Joseph Heinzen, there is no public structure on the North Shore like it or that so clearly reflects the area's early history.

The first floor housed the fire department, police department and the Village trustee meetings. The second floor was used for community dances and parties. The Village Hall was the center of lively village life.

Most of Gross Point's income was derived from taxes garnered from its 15 taverns and saloons. Gross Point saloons were targeted by the Evanston's Citizen League for violation of an ordinance prohibiting sale of liquor within four miles of Northwestern University campus. Prohibition dealt the death blow to Gross Point.

In April 1919, the citizens of Gross Point voted to dissolve their government and the Gross Point Village Hall was sold to pay village debts. In 1924, Gross Point was annexed by Wilmette.

Even though this proud building has suffered unfortunate remodeling, its integrity is sufficiently intact to someday allow a sensitive restoration to capture the building's important historic identity.

Chicago and North Western Railroad Passenger Depot
1135 Wilmette Avenue
Wilmette, Illinois

Built in 1873, the Victorian style Chicago and North Western Depot is one of Wilmette's oldest and most historically significant buildings. It is thought to have been designed by the railroad. Ten major landowners and developers paid nearly $3,500 to construct the new station to impress prospective land buyers from Chicago. The Chicago "Sunday Times," May 4, 1873, called the Wilmette Depot "a pretentious affair...the finest station on the entire line."

Although intended to be functional, the buff-colored brick depot has elegant detailing. Its gently sloping roof creates a deep porch to protect passengers from rain while waiting for the train. The overhang is supported by gracefully curved brackets extending from square columns. Brackets and wood trim were originally painted black with decorative incised details traced in gold leaf.

Brickwork is crisp and particularly handsome. On each gable end of the building are stepped corbels. Shouldered pediments or hoodmolds top the recessed arched windows.

The ticketmaster's bay projects beyond the plane of the wall, allowing a view of approaching trains. Tall, narrow windows and a cornice ornamented by dentils are typical Victorian details.

The station, after being replaced in 1896, was moved to the north and used as a freight depot for many years. In 1972, threatened with demolition, the Wilmette Historical Society led a campaign to save it. The 1873 Chicago and North Western Railroad Depot was moved to its present location for creative adaptive reuse and carefully restored. It was placed on the National Register of Historic Places in 1980.

Asahel Gage House
1134 Elmwood Avenue
Wilmette, Illinois

The Asahel Gage house reflects 19th Century Victorian Italianate architecture. A blend of classical and romantic elements, this structure is an eclectic copy of a Tuscan farmhouse. The pastoral life represented by the Italianate style held great appeal during the Industrial Revolution. Storybook villas were adapted and built by architects in England and by craftsmen in the United States.

The Gage house was built in 1873. It was designed by T. V. Wadski and built by Horace and Edwin Drury. Typical of Italianate houses, the gabled roofs, often more steeply pitched in the Midwest to shed snow, have wide eaves supported by ornamental paired brackets. A distinctive four-story entrance tower with a steep mansard roof is topped by cast iron cresting. Although many Italianate homes had towers, few have survived. The open veranda, projecting bay and tall narrow windows with pedimented hoodmolds are characteristically Victorian.

The Gage family was important in the development of Wilmette and Winnetka. New Yorker John Gage purchased two large tracts of land, one in what was Ouilmette Reservation and the other between Kenilworth and Wilmette. Ouilmette Reservation was 1,280 acres of land given by the government to Archange Ouilmette and her husband, Antoine, for help with the Treaty of Prairie du Chien in 1829. This treaty was the beginning of the push to oust the Indians from Illinois and Wisconsin. Archange Ouilmette was half Potawatomi Indian.

Years later many city residents sought safety after Chicago's Great Fire of 1871 on large tracts of land away from congestion. Asahel Gage, son of John Gage, recognized this trend and platted his father's lush wooded property. In 1875 he began promotion of "Gage's Addition" to Wilmette featuring this house.

The Asahel Gage house has been authentically restored utilizing several colors, as the Victorians did, that accentuate its details. Even the sparse landscaping with few ground plantings is characteristically Victorian.

Frank Scheidenhelm House
804 Forest Avenue
Wilmette, Illinois

From 1900 to 1920 American Foursquare houses were built by the thousands all over the United States. The basic Foursquare was symmetrical. It stood two stories over a raised basement with the first floor reached by steps. A broad porch stretched across the front. The house was usually capped by a hipped roof with a central dormer. As implied by the name, the basic floor plan was a box divided into four equal-sized rooms on each floor.

The Foursquare developed as a reaction against the Victorian styles, particularly the Queen Anne. Although usually more modest, its massive solid form is not very different in shape from the Colonial Revival style also popular during this period.

Foursquares, like variations on a musical theme, lent themselves to many stylistic interpretations. Some were tall and imposing, a reminder of the Victorians built during the last decade of the 19th Century. Like this house, some stretched into the surrounding landscape, clearly Prairie School in their horizontal expanse.

Built in 1902, this beautifully proportioned Foursquare house was designed by Kenilworth architect George Washington Maher. The intricate Sullivanesque ornamental trim around the arched dormer and porch columns make it distinctive. The typical Foursquare was not architect-designed, and, in fact, could be purchased from mail order companies.

The Foursquare became a very popular style in most North Shore villages, but Wilmette residents seemed to have a special fondness for it. They are found in every variation, with English, Spanish, Prairie or Classical details.

Edward R. Scheidenhelm House
704 Lake Avenue
Wilmette, Illinois

The architectural firm of Tallmadge and Watson designed this handsome Prairie School residence in 1911. The house was built for Edward and Harriet Scheidenhelm. Edward Scheidenhelm, a civil engineer, was a well-known Chicago contractor. His most famous project was Chicago's Municipal (Navy) Pier. Harriet Scheidenhelm was a prominent horticulturalist and landscaper.

Thomas Eddy Tallmadge (1876-1940) and Vernon S. Watson (1879-1950) met while working as draftsmen for Daniel H. Burnham, chief architect of the World's Columbian Exposition of 1893. They established a long-lasting partnership in 1905. Its focus was on residential and church architecture.

Tallmadge and Watson designed several houses on the North Shore, many of which were Tudor in inspiration although Tudor design elements were highly abstracted. Where Tudor forms are borrowed they are disciplined and convey a horizontal rather than vertical emphasis. In this house, a front facing gable is prominent and half-timbering is suggested in the window treatment, but these are clearly read as geometric, not Tudor, design features. This is a Prairie house.

The Scheidenhelm house contains many Prairie School elements. It has carefully articulated rose brickwork, broad overhanging eaves and horizontal stone banding. Especially noteworthy is the three-part window with fine Prairie School stained glass set into the third story gable. This is a Tallmadge and Watson trait evident in many of their house designs on the North Shore.

The Alfred Bersbach House

1120 Michigan Avenue
Wilmette, Illinois

Constructed in 1914, the Alfred Bersbach house is considered one of architect John S. Van Bergen's most originally detailed works. Wrightian in derivation, it has been praised as carefully proportioned and professionally executed.

The Bersbach house epitomizes the Prairie School in its long, low, horizontal appearance, wood banding and flat roof with wide overhanging eaves. Like many Prairie School buildings, the main floor is raised above ground level. Leaded glass casement windows provide large expanses of glass overlooking Lake Michigan.

John Van Bergen was born in Oak Park, Illinois, in 1885. Architect Walter Burley Griffin, an Oak Park neighbor, hired young Van Bergen for his Steinway Hall office in Chicago even though Van Bergen had no previous architectural training. Later, Van Bergen worked for Frank Lloyd Wright and was, in fact, the last employee hired before Wright closed his office in the autumn of 1909 and left for Europe. William Drummond, Wright's chief draftsman, and Van Bergen completed Wright's work. Van Bergen supervised several projects under construction, allowing no changes to be made to Wright's plans.

John Van Bergen established his private practice in Ravinia, Illinois, (now Highland Park) after World War I. He built his home across the ravine from prominent Prairie landscape architect and naturalist, Jens Jensen. No doubt influenced by Jensen, Van Bergen's designs became more rustic and natural, incorporating the use of rough-faced limestone.

Throughout his long and productive career, John Van Bergen designed in the Prairie School idiom. Even after 1920, when historical styles became popular, he was still able to secure commissions for Prairie School buildings, doing so into the 1930s, long after the style was abandoned by Wright. John Van Bergen died at age 84 in 1964.

Ralph S. Baker House
1226 Ashland Avenue
Wilmette, Illinois

The Baker house, an exceptional Prairie School residence, is considered William Drummond's most refined work. It was designed in 1914 for Ralph S. Baker, an auditor with Chicago Tool Co., by the firm of Guenzel & Drummond. Drummond created a stark and simple interpretation of Prairie School architecture using long rectangular forms, slab roofs, strips of casement windows and stucco walls trimmed with wood bands. Like Frank Lloyd Wright, Drummond incorporated patterned leaded windows into his designs.

William Eugene Drummond was born in Newark, New Jersey in 1876. Although lacking formal education, he joined the Frank Lloyd Wright Oak Park studio in 1899 and remained until 1909. Drummond was greatly respected by Wright and at times was his chief draftsman. After he left Wright's office, Drummond went into private practice from 1909-1912, a period that was creative and fruitful.

In 1912 Drummond joined Louis Guenzel to form the firm Guenzel and Drummond. Louis Guenzel was born in Caselin, Germany in 1860. He came to the United States to work in the office of Adler and Sullivan. In 1894 he worked in Wright's studio, later established his own practice, then allied with Drummond. In the Guenzel and Drummond partnership, Louis Guenzel was business manager; Drummond provided the design expertise.

Two tragic events ended the five year partnership and both architects' hopes of future success. The first was the outbreak of World War I and its anti-German sentiments. The second, which also marked the demise of the Prairie School, was the murder of Wright's companion, Mamah Cheney, and six others in connection with the burning of Wright's Taliesin studio by a berserk servant. Exploitation by the newspapers created a lengthy scandal for Wright and his followers. The Prairie School movement virtually fell apart when many architects, including Wright, left Chicago.

G. J. Bichl House
Wilmette, Illinois

Built in 1923 by the firm of George Washington Maher and Son, this yellow brick mansion and the similiar house next door were designed by the son, Philip Maher. The houses were built by a father for his two daughters and are connected by a tunnel. The two homes share a swimming pool.

The elegant G. J. Bichl House has historical references in its molded Tudor chimneys with chimney pots, leaded glass and diamond brickwork. Yet these characteristics are so abstracted, so stripped down, that the building appears almost modern in its sophisticated severity.

Philip Brooks Maher, born in 1894 in Kenilworth, Illinois, studied architecture at the University of Michigan. He worked in his father's successful firm from 1914 to 1924, then established his own practice in 1924. As his career developed, he became a modernist, striving for simplicity.

Some important Chicago buildings attributable to Philip Maher are the Woman's Athletic Club, the Art Deco high rise apartment building at 1301 Astor Street and the Saks Fifth Avenue Building on Michigan Avenue.

Philip Maher's architecture shows strength and power. Although rooted in the past, it exhibits his father's influence in its tendency toward geometric abstraction. Philip Maher had the ability to draw from Classical or medieval precedents, absorb the influence of his father's architecture and create a personal synthesis that appealed to a fashionable clientele.

The John Burns House
1708 Lake Avenue
Wilmette, Illinois

Assertively modern, the John Burns house was built in 1938. R.W. Stott, architect, designed this impressive example of Art Deco architecture, one of only a few North Shore buildings that can truly be called Art Deco.

Art Deco takes its name from the 1925 Paris "Exposition Internationale des Arts Decoratifs et Industriels Modernes." Literature from the Exposition promoted originality and strictly prohibited entries that were "reproductions, imitation and counterfeits of ancient style." Art Deco emphasized the future and sought to embody the machine age with mass produced, artistically-designed items. Art Deco influenced the look of clothing, furniture, household goods, sculpture and paintings. Although it penetrated the decorative arts, the style rarely broke the stronghold historicism had on architecture.

Breaking with the Beaux Arts and Revivalist styles, Art Deco was the first new style to gain wide popularity in the United States. It reached its height in the 1930s.

America, ever worshipful of automobiles, airplanes and modern oceanliners, began in the late 1930s to streamline its buildings. To suggest speed flow, houses such as this used "racing stripes" and porthole windows. An exceptionally fine detail on 1708 Lake Avenue is the sweeping, semicircular, stainless steel canopy over the front door. Integrated into this Art Deco design are such International Style features as flat roofs, planar surfaces and corner windows. Like contemporary International Style buildings, it relies on geometry for its design inspiration.

Notable examples of Art Deco architecture include the Chrysler Building and Radio City Music Hall in New York City and the small sherbet-colored hotels in the Miami Beach Art Deco Historic District.

Herbert Bruning House
2716 Blackhawk Road
Wilmette, Illinois

International Style architecture on the North Shore is well represented by the Herbert Bruning house designed in 1937 by George Fred Keck. It displays a sophisticated use of concrete, glass and steel, rejecting non-essential ornamentation in favor of stark simplicity. The prototypical International Style house has flat roofs and planar surfaces. It represents an exercise in geometry. The porch and chimney addition merely add new geometric elements.

Reminiscent of Keck's ultra-modern House of Tomorrow and Crystal House from the Century of Progress International Exposition of 1933-1934, the Bruning house incorporates many of the same innovative features. These amenities included the latest mechanical equipment for heating and air conditioning and an all-electric kitchen.

The steel-framed, reinforced concrete house has 15 rooms. A passive solar cylindrical glass block tower floods the interior circular stairway with light and warmth.

George Fred Keck and younger brother William were born in Watertown, Wisconsin. Both attended the University of Illinois at Urbana. William Keck joined George Fred Keck's firm, established in 1926, as a full partner in 1937. Their practice remained largely residential. William Keck took over guidance of the firm after his brother's death.

Keck and Keck, in the forefront of modern architecture, experimented with solar energy, prefabrication and low maintenance techniques.

In 1979, the Kecks were honored at the fourth National Passive Solar Conference as "solar pioneers." They synthesized old ideas with new materials in a revolutionary way and created a substantial number of handsome and livable buildings.

Kenilworth Railroad Station
Kenilworth Avenue & Green Bay Road
Kenilworth, Illinois

Kenilworth dates from 1889 when Joseph Sears formed the Kenilworth Company to develop 225 acres between the villages of Wilmette and Winnetka. While it was a business venture for an investors' syndicate, its founders were dedicated to creating an exclusive community of families they considered acceptable and of high standards. This early experiment in town planning was aimed at promoting top quality construction, maintaining a homogeneous character and preventing haphazard development. Even though fully improved lots in Kenilworth sold for roughly four times that of lots outside the community, the Kenilworth Company reached its goal of 300 residents rapidly. The Kenilworth Company was then disbanded and in 1896, the Village of Kenilworth was incorporated.

The name Kenilworth was sentimentally chosen by Joseph Sears after a family trip to Kenilworth in Warwickshire, England. Many Kenilworth street names are drawn from the characters and places featured in a romantic novel of the same name by Sir Walter Scott.

Since the Kenilworth Company was in business to sell expensive lots, construction of the train station was a priority. Franklin Burnham, Kenilworth Company architect and director (no relationship to Daniel H. Burnham), was charged with designing a structure suitable to the Kenilworth concept. For his station design, Burnham chose the popular Richardsonian Romanesque style. Boston architect H. H. Richardson developed the style and often used it in designs for railroad stations outside of Boston. The style is loosely derived from Romanesque architecture. It is characterized by rough-faced masonry, in this case sandstone, round-headed arches and an overall massiveness. In the station, the Richardsonian Romanesque elements form a deep veranda surrounding the waiting rooms and ticket office, making the small building appear larger and more imposing.

The station was rehabilitated in the early 1980s.

Ullman Strong House

321 Melrose Avenue
Kenilworth, Illinois

After the 1893 World's Columbian Exposition in Chicago, Kenilworth tradition has it that Ullman Strong hired the German craftsmen who built that country's pavilion to construct his Kenilworth home. Corroborating this tale is the Germanic atmosphere of the high Victorian interior, where warm, fine-grained white oak was used for extensive paneling and massive hand-carved newel posts, cabinetry and mantles.

The architect of this typical Queen Anne style house, completed in 1896, is unknown. It is a large, irregular-shaped house with a steeply-pitched front gable. The irregular roofline emphasized by the seven prominent chimneys is typical Queen Anne. Various roof levels and multiple roof shapes contribute to the massing of the house. These rooflines, juxtaposed with fairly flat porch and porte cochere roofs and two partial turrets, result in a visually rich structure.

Rich, varied surface texture is another Queen Anne trait. The four-foot high foundation was constructed of yellow rough-faced sandstone, providing a firm visual base to the house. The first story is sheathed in thin horizontal clapboards, originally painted a dark red to add further visual weight. The second and third stories are of various shaped shingles and were painted a creamy yellow by the builders. Accents of black and dark green further enlivened the original look of the house.

The Ullman Strong house is situated on a corner lot appropriate to the scale of the home. A coachhouse echos the design elements of the main house. Later owners, collectors of rare botanical specimens, installed an intricate wrought iron fence around the property to protect the collection. It was reportedly the first fence in Kenilworth and was controversial at the time.

James A. Culbertson House
220 Melrose Avenue
Kenilworth, Illinois

Franklin Burnham, architect for the village's developer, the Kenilworth Company, designed this Queen Anne style house in 1893. It was built for James Culbertson, who moved from Kentucky seeking a residence nearer his Michigan lumber interests. Culbertson is said to have selected a ravine lot because of its trees. The use of various woods inside the house reflects its first owner's love of the material.

Culbertson was one of Kenilworth's most distinguished early citizens. He served as first president of the Kenilworth Club, 1894-1895, and as first village president, 1896-1897. The Kenilworth Union Church, to which he donated a gymnasium and guild room, and the Kenilworth Club, for which he donated one-half the funds for construction, were beneficiaries of his generosity.

Taking the basic Queen Anne structure, with its imposing size, picturesque massing and wrap-around porch, Burnham developed several historical themes. Most obvious is the half-timbering characteristic of Tudor architecture. The grid of timbers and stucco adds ornamental surface treatment, a typical Queen Anne characteristic, to the second and third floors. Softening the rather rigid geometric effect is a graceful, floral motif of garlands, ribbons, and rosettes. This French "Watteau-esque" element is used in the ornamental stucco frieze between the second and third floors and highlights the gables and dormers. The first floor is of yellow sandstone, a favorite material of Burnham and the Kenilworth Company. In keeping with the weighted look of the stone, paired Tuscan columns support the porch roof. These various historically-derived design elements contribute to the eclecticism often typical of Queen Anne architecture.

Dr. Charles Smith House
258 Melrose Avenue
Kenilworth, Illinois

This Shingle style house was the second home built in Kenilworth for Dr. Charles Smith, secretary of the Kenilworth Company that developed the town. He broke ground on his new residence in 1895 and moved from 339 Kenilworth Avenue the following year. Among Dr. Smith's most lasting contributions to the village was his design of the Kenilworth logo. Executed in his highly-stylized back-sloping handwriting, it was copied for the railroad station sign in 1891.

Evolving from Queen Anne architecture, the Shingle style is similar but considerably quieter and less complicated in its massing. Details are subdued and tend to emphasize the horizontal. It takes its name from the building's most characteristic feature, the shingled surface. Use of a gambrel roof is typical.

The Smith house demonstrates an almost contemporary clarity in its Shingle style design. It has a gently flared gambrel roof, punctuated by a row of dormers. This is dramatically balanced by a sweeping circular two-story tower, providing a focal point for the entrance. The rustic simplicity of shingles is elegantly accented by a series of Corinthian columns on the tower that are proportioned to give an impression of strength and solidity. The building's emphatic horizontal lines suggested by the windows and columns of the tower, the division between first and second stories, and the deep flared overhangs of the dormers and tower are typical stylistic characteristics of Shingle style buildings. The architect for this house is not known.

Shingle style architecture became popular in the 1880s and 1890s in summer homes. Derived from Colonial shingled houses in New England seaside villages, the style remains associated with suburban or resort life.

Frank Root House

326 Essex Road
Kenilworth, Illinois

"Make no small plans" was the creed of Daniel Burnham, internationally famous architect and early city planner who designed this Classical Revival style house in 1896 for music publisher, Frank Root.

Classical Revival architecture tended to be reserved for prominent public buildings such as banks, museums and village halls. It is used less often for private residences. This house, designed by the style's originator, is a masterpiece. The four great Ionic portico columns were said to be "left over" from the Court of Honor at the World's Columbian Exposition of 1893. Other Classical details include pilasters, urns, curved pediments, dentils and balustrades all integrated to form an elegant symmetry.

Burnham is best remembered in Chicago as coordinating architect of the World's Columbian Exposition of 1893. Drawing heavily from historical precedents, especially Classical Greek, Burnham was responsible for the classicism of "The White City." Following the Exposition, the Classical Revival style swept the country. A lasting result was the conviction that all clapboard buildings, regardless of style, should be painted white.

Burnham's career was to blossom. In 1901, he headed the commission to extend L'Enfant's layout for Washington, D.C. In 1909 he devised the famous Chicago Plan and by 1910 D. H. Burnham & Associates was the largest architectural firm in the world.

Burnham's numerous architectural achievements include The Rookery (Chicago, 1885), the Monadnock Building (Chicago, 1891), the Reliance Building (Chicago, 1894), the Flatiron Building (New York, 1901), Marshall Field & Company (Chicago, 1902), and Selfridge's Department Store (London, England, 1906).

The builder who executed Burnham's design was Kenilworth resident Paul Starrett, a World's Columbian Exposition contractor, who later worked with Burnham as builder of the Flatiron Building and the Lincoln Memorial (Washington, D.C., 1911) and built the Empire State Building (New York, 1931).

Kenilworth Union Church
211 Kenilworth Avenue
Kenilworth, Illinois

In 1892, when denominational interests and religious differences were of paramount significance, the early residents of Kenilworth, under the leadership of Joseph Sears, founded the first nondenominational community church in America. The church united in one fellowship members of all Protestant denominations.

The Kenilworth Company had its architect, Franklin Burnham, designer of the train station, draw up plans. Burnham selected the Gothic Revival style, appropriately inspired by the cathedrals of the Christian medieval past. The church was built of the same rough-faced sandstone Burnham used for the train station. In addition, he designed three residences along Kenilworth Avenue using the distinctive yellow Sandstone: 354, 339, and 37 Kenilworth Avenue, his own home.

The theme of unity among the Protestant denominations is emphasized throughout the building. Nine denominations — Methodist, Baptist, Lutheran, Congregational, Episcopal, Presbyterian, Disciples of Christ, Quakers and Swedenborgians, or church of the New Jerusalem — are depicted in the stained glass windows of the sanctuary. These windows were a major feature of the rebuilding program undertaken in 1949. They are made of imported antique glass of the same kind used in European cathedrals in the 13th and 14th Centuries.

Two major Gothic style additions to the exterior were built in the 1950s. Rising above the northwest corner of the sanctuary is a high copper steeple that provides a vertical counterpoint to the building's silhouette. The cloister walk is a colonnade of Gothic arches. In its pillars are stones from important places in the history of Christianity.

George W. Maher House
424 Warwick Road
Kenilworth, Illinois

George Maher's own home, built in 1893, is a blend of Arts and Crafts, Swiss chalet, Chinese, Scandinavian and Gothic styles. This fanciful and airy design has a flared, steeply-pitched roof with dormers on each side, capped by painted copper finials.

The interior is surprising with its open plan and geometric Prairie School ornamentation. Massive plain wood columns instead of walls suggest room boundaries.

The house was influenced by the Arts and Crafts movement which started with the work of William Morris in mid-Victorian England. It gained popularity in the United States and in Chicago after 1897 when the Arts and Crafts Society was founded at Hull House. It greatly influenced Society member Frank Lloyd Wright and the architects of the Prairie School. In a typical Arts and Crafts house, the windows and bays are placed according to need rather than because of formal considerations. This is true here where the windows are varied in placement, size and shape. Many feature a leaded diamond pattern.

Maher, born in 1864 in West Virginia, began his study of architecture at age 13 when he apprenticed in the architectural office of August Bauer and Henry W. Hill. He soon joined the firm of J.L. Silsbee where Frank Lloyd Wright worked as a draftsman.

In 1888, at age 23, with opinions on architecture firmly established, Maher opened his own firm. He successfully designed buildings using his interpretation of Prairie School architecture even when historical revival styles were commonplace. Throughout his career he assimilated ideas and synthesized various architectural influences, ultimately developing a style that emphasized massiveness, symmetry and variations on a dominent ornamental motif.

Maher married Elizabeth Brooks and had one son, Philip Brooks Maher, who also achieved acclaim for his architecture. The Maher family lived in Kenilworth, Ilinois, where George Maher designed many Prairie School houses.

Frank G. Ely House
305 Kenilworth Avenue
Kenilworth, Illinois

The Frank G. Ely house, designed by Maher in 1908, is a typical George Maher Prairie School design. A foremost Maher signature is the repetition of the segmental arch motif found in the house.

Architect George Washington Maher's "motive-rhythm theory" used a single decorative theme to unify a structure both internally and externally. This decorative concept had little to do with functional design. An example was the use of the thistle applied throughout the 1901 Evanston residence of James A. Patten (demolished). The often repeated thistle appeared on walls, ceiling, draperies, table scarves and was carved on woodwork, mantles and furniture. Later, Maher substituted architectural motifs for floral ones.

In the Frank G. Ely house, built in 1908, Maher repeats the segmental arch. It seems to appear everywhere. It caps piers and doorways and appears over the second-story dormer windows, the entrance and the chimney caps. The motif is frequently repeated in interior details such as banisters and newel posts.

The Ely house is representative of Maher's style in its symmetrical, rectangular shape, canted walls and broad hipped roof with overhanging eaves. This basic design is easily recognized in many North Shore houses designed by Maher.

F. Lackner House
521 Roslyn Road
Kenilworth, Illinois

George W. Maher developed a fairly consistant, disciplined style as his career progressed. He was heavily influenced by Frank Lloyd Wright's William H. Winslow House of 1893. However, this house and its next door neighbor, the F.M. Corbin House at 533 Roslyn Road, both built around 1904, display a different side of Maher's design ingenuity. He was clearly experimenting with a building's shape, as well as its ornamentation.

The Lackner house reflects Maher's interest in European architecture, specifically the turn of the century Austrian Secessionist movement. Secessionist architecture was the Viennese version of Art Nouveau. The Secessionists were searching for an appropriate style for the modern age. It was often expressed in simple structures with organic ornamentation disciplined by geometry. Maher's curiosity about Secessionist buildings was kindled in 1904 after a visit to the Louisiana Purchase Exposition in St. Louis. Maher was impressed by the Secessionist work displayed there.

Secessionist influence is seen in the use of stucco, plain flat surfaces, crisp lines and the building's overall shape. The Lackner House closely resembles a house designed by Secessionist architect, Josef Hoffman in 1899. Today it is Hoffman's furniture designs that have become popular.

Despite Viennese influence, the segmental arch is a telling Maher hallmark. In the Ely House at 305 Kenilworth Avenue (1908), the arch is used repeatedly to express his motive-rhythm theory. In the Lackner and Corbin houses it is one of several features contributing to the building's highly original design.

Maher's ability to absorb various stylistic influences, struggle with them and create his version of the modern house is immediately evident in his Lackner house design.

Kenilworth Club
410 Kenilworth Avenue
Kenilworth, Illinois

The Kenilworth Club, originally known as the Kenilworth Assembly Hall Association, is a community civic organization and a private social club offering a calendar of events for residents. Founded in 1894, the Assembly Hall dues were $10 for men, to be paid semi-annually, and $2.50 for women. Prominent architect George W. Maher, a Kenilworth resident, was commissioned to design the clubhouse.

Built in 1907, the Kenilworth Club is in the Prairie School style. It is a low, one-story building with strong horizontal lines and wide overhanging eaves. Walls are of white stucco ornamented with vertical strips of wood set in an abstracted geometric design.

Exceptional stained glass windows contain an angular vertical design of clear glass topped by a diamond featuring a stylized symbol of a tree in green glass and Lake Michigan in blue glass. The same symbol was stenciled on the interior walls.

Originally the Kenilworth Club had an enormous American elm tree projecting through an opening in the entranceway roof. It was a dramatic feature lost when the tree died of Dutch Elm disease in 1976.

Important in Maher's early career, the Kenilworth Club is one of his last designs with horizontal emphasis. In this building, as well as others, Maher worked on juxtaposing vertical elements against horizontal Prairie School lines. This building is listed on the National Register of Historic Places.

Mahoney Park Council Ring
Sheridan Road
Kenilworth, Illinois

Land for Mahoney Park, 3.12 acres overlooking Lake Michigan, was willed to the Village of Kenilworth in 1933 by pioneer descendant, Mary Mahoney. Jens Jensen, prominent Prairie landscape architect, was asked to design this small, intimate park.

Born in Denmark, Jensen immigrated to the United States in 1883, settling in Chicago in 1886. Along with William LeBaron Jenney, Daniel H. Burnham and Frederick Law Olmsted (who designed New York City's Central Park), he is credited as a major designer of Chicago's park system. He worked his way up to superintendent of the West Park system where he was responsible for the design of Garfield, Douglas, Columbus and Humboldt Parks. Jensen continued on and off with the Chicago Park System until 1920. At the same time he maintained a private practice designing large country estates.

The commission for Mahoney Park probably appealed to Jensen because residents of Kenilworth desired a sanctuary for birds and wildflowers. He chose to enhance, rather than change, the natural environment. He was a nature poet, father of the Prairie style of landscape design. Using the horizontal feeling of the prairie as inspiration, he chose plants with strong horizontal branching, created streams that curved and flowed like the prairie rivers and planted masses of flowers that painted the horizon with subtle colors and shading.

In Mahoney Park, Jensen combined the broad expanse of the meadow with flowing borders of native plantings and curved stone paths to create a peaceful, natural setting. He incorporated into this design seven semi-circular council rings as an invitation to sit quietly in contemplation or join one's neighbors in friendly conversation. The council ring was Jensen's design signature.

Private Residence
270 Scott Avenue
Winnetka, Illinois

Only a few Victorian Gothic houses exist on the North Shore, and this one is noteworthy because of its fine detailing. Its lacy bargeboard, pointed arch windows, steep gables and door canopy are a master carpenter's interpretation of Gothic architecture. Like all Carpenter Gothic buildings, it represents a loose, romantic vision of the medieval Gothic cathedral translated into wood.

Victorian Gothic architecture was part of the romantic movement that permeated the art, music and literature of the 19th Century. One aspect was the intense interest in the virtues of the Christian medieval past, so romantics happily fostered the revival of Gothic architecture. Still, it never achieved widespread popularity. Because of its strong association with the church and the English aristocracy, Victorian Gothic architecture was not generally acknowledged as a suitable expression of American democracy.

Victorian Gothic cottages can be found throughout the country, largely because of the wide circulation of pattern books in the 1850s and 1860s. Plans for the houses of Alexander Jackson Davis, America's most prolific proponent of the style, were published in "Cottage Residences" by Davis' friend Andrew Jackson Downing, whose pattern books had a tremendous impact on the shaping of 19th Century architectural taste. It is likely that the design for 270 Scott Avenue was taken from one of these books. The contemporary invention of the power-driven jigsaw and lathe and the easy availability of wood enabled the local carpenter to convert such designs into reality.

The structure at 270 Scott Avenue was built in the 1860s as a summer house. It was part of an enclave of buildings surrounding what was, in the 1850s and 1860s, the settlement of Taylorsport. Today it is one of the small group of Victorians remaining, a handsome reminder of Winnetka's 19th Century roots.

William Augustis Otis House
644 Oak Street
Winnetka, Illinois

The house that William Augustis Otis designed for his own family about 1890 can only be described as eclectic. Its overall shape, with a steep front gable, is reminiscent of the Victorian Gothic style popular on the North Shore in the late 1860s. Its molded chimney and third-floor bay window with leaded transoms recall medieval architecture and suggests the English Tudor style that emerged in popularity in the early 1900s and peaked in the 1920s. The building's emphatic horizontal design, flared roofline and simple uniform surface treatment associate it with the Shingle style that emerged in the 1880s in East Coast resort towns. The Shingle style grew out of the Queen Anne, but is quieter and less complicated in shape, use of materials and ornamental treatment. The design of 644 Oak Street may not be related to any one particular style, but is a sophisticated example of the many 19th Century houses that combine influences.

William Augustis Otis was a well-trained, highly-respected architect. He grew up in New York and received an architectural education at the University of Michigan (1874-1877) and the École des Beaux Arts in Paris (1877-1881), where his training was grounded in the study of historic architecture. When he returned to the United States in 1882, he joined the firm of Chicago School architect, William LeBaron Jenney, and became his partner in 1887. Otis, in 1909, joined Edwin H. Clark, who later designed Winnetka's Village Hall. Otis served as a lecturer in architectural history at The Art Institute of Chicago and designed a number of North Shore buildings. His work includes the University Club in Evanston, Lunt Hall and Music Hall on the Northwestern University campus, Christ Church in Winnetka and numerous residences.

Private Residence
577 Cherry Street
Winnetka, Illinois

Colonial Revival architecture, referring to a renewed interest in houses built along the Eastern seaboard between 1750 and 1820, took different forms. Sometimes the inspiration was Georgian, Dutch Colonial, or Federal. The World's Columbian Exposition of 1893 heightened North Shore interest in Colonial Revival architecture. Called the White City, this world's fair was a Classical tour de force. When Classicism filtered down to residential architecture, it was translated into the less formal Colonial Revival.

The Philadelphia Centennial Exhibition of 1876 is credited with establishing an interest in America's early Colonial roots. The style associated with America's history had a symbolic significance and enormous nostalgic appeal. It felt comfortable. Colonial Revival ultimately became the country's most popular architectural style.

The house at 577 Cherry Street, built in 1900, is a very early example of the Federal Revival aspect of Colonial Revival architecture. Like others built in the first decade of the 20th Century, its design closely approximates the proportions and detailing of actual Federal style residences. It is not very different from the mansions of a Salem ship captain or a Providence banker.

Federal architecture dominated American building on the Atlantic coast between 1790 and 1820. It grew out of the preceding Georgian style, employed similar Classical detailing but was considerably more refined in proportion and ornamental trim. This structure beautifully exemplifies the Federal style revived. It stands three stories over a raised basement. Classical detailing includes a gracious front portico, delicate fluted pilasters framing the house and pedimented dormers. A less typical feature is the roof's Chinese Chippendale balustrade topped by Roman urns. There is no more elegant example of Federal Revival architecture on the North Shore.

Winnetka Village Hall
510 Green Bay Road
Winnetka, Illinois

The Village Hall of Winnetka, with Classical symmetry and Georgian detailing, reflects civic architecture as envisioned by Daniel H. Burnham and Edward H. Bennett better than any other North Shore public building. In 1909 these two men co-authored the Chicago Plan, which the city officially adopted for economic and physical development. Chicago owes its formal front yard, the Neoclassically designed Grant Park, and its industry-free lakefront to the Burnham Plan.

Edward H. Bennett, Burnham's co-author, had a significant impact on Winnetka. He served as consulting architect on the Winnetka Plan of 1921. Prominent in the plan are his comments on the location of the Village Hall. It was to be in the center of the block west of the railroad station, with a triangular park in the front facing the station and a symmetrical open mall to the rear. Designed in 1925, it fits into the surroundings in a carefully planned, orderly way.

The Village Hall building has a pedimented center entrance topped by a graceful cupola and flanked by symmetrical wings. Classically inspired Georgian details emphasize its significance. Burnham contended that Classicism best expressed the symbolic importance of government. European examples include the Acropolis in Athens and the Forum in Rome. In the United States, government buildings in Washington set the standard.

Village resident and architect Edwin H. Clark designed the Winnetka Village Hall. To quote Lora Townsend Dickenson in "The Story of Winnetka," "The Village Hall is attractive in appearance—not cold and forbidding, but much like a beautiful home. One notes the fine proportions of the building, its simplicity and warm dignity, its adherence to governmental architecture—the north wing, the south wing and the central modified dome."

Edwin Clark is remembered as the architect in charge of site planning and building design at Brookfield Zoo, built 1926-1934.

The Chimneys
158 Green Bay Road
Winnetka, Illinois

Unlike any multi-family dwelling on the North Shore, the layout of the Chimneys, built in 1929, is patterned after an actual London Street. Built around a narrow secluded courtyard, it is clearly Tudor. The steep projecting roof gables, half-timbering and multi-paned windows are typical characteristics of the Tudor Revival style popular in the 1920s. Like most other Tudor buildings of the period, it attempts stylistic accuracy.

Practically all residences on the North Shore, whether Victorian, historical revival or modern in style, are single family. Only Evanston has a proliferation of apartment buildings. In the other cities and villages, apartment living is centered in the business district and usually located over first floor shops. The Chimneys, an apartment complex, is three stories that appear to be two because of the gabled roofline. It looks more like a string of houses.

The Chimneys was developed by attorney Roland D. Whitman, who lived nearby. It was convenient to the train station and provided amenities to satisfy any homeowner: working fireplaces, hardwood floors and screen porches. Pleasant, small-scale entries open off the courtyard to the apartments, and each unit has sound-proof construction. The architect is thought to have been S.S. Beman Jr. who also designed Whitman's own house. Beman is responsible for many fine houses and Christian Science churches on the North Shore. The builder was Edward A. Anderson & Co. Established in 1913, this contracting company built several North Shore structures including the Bob O'Link Golf Club in Highland Park and the Ayers Boal Building at 723 Elm Street in Winnetka. The firm still exists under Anderson family ownership.

Felix Lowy House
140 Sheridan Road
Winnetka, Illinois

This stately English manor house was designed by the architectural firm of Mayo and Mayo in 1925. It is representative of the Winnetka mansions along Sheridan Road, which wends its way along Lake Michigan through the entire North Shore. Although the house's large parcel of property has been subdivided, its stately front yard has been appropriately retained. The house is large, impressive and derivative of Tudor architecture.

Tudor was a favored style in the 1920s, employed for private homes, college dormitories and commercial buildings. It was especially popular in North Shore town centers, where the most architecturally cohesive areas were designed to have the look of quiet, dignified English villages. But it was also favored to lend respectability to residences and was well-suited to this 16-room house of Felix Lowy, vice president of Colgate-Palmolive. Its brick masonry facades, steep front-facing gables, slate roof and tall leaded windows are typical Tudor features.

Ernest Mayo was born in England in 1868 and, although not a household name, he designed several administration buildings for the World's Columbian Exposition of 1893 and many large North Shore houses. His residential designs are found throughout Evanston, where he lived. Peter, his son, joined the firm in 1918, which then became known as Mayo and Mayo. The Lowy house is a splendid representation of their work.

Max Epstein House
Edgecliffe
915 Sheridan Road
Winnetka, Illinois

Like many designs by architect Samuel Marx, the 1930 Max Epstein house combines historic traditionalism with the pared-down simplicity of modernism. Marx looked to French domestic architecture for inspiration.

From Sheridan Road the mansion is framed by two identical symmetrical gatehouses, each entered through a doorway topped by a delicate wrought iron canopy and each with a flared mansard roof, the French hallmark. The elegant, almost processional, formality of the approach to the house is also typically French.

Equally interesting is the modernity of the buildings. Their French characteristics are abstracted and highly disciplined. The color scheme is muted; facades are of buff-colored brick. There is no applied ornament. The overall shape of the gatehouses is simple and geometric; each is a basic box. Edges are crisp, surfaces are flat and lines are simple. The main house reflects similar stylistic influences.

Samuel Marx, born in 1885, had classical architectural training. He studied at Massachusetts Institute of Technology and the École de Beaux Arts in Paris. Although he went into practice in 1909, his career peaked in the 1930s and 1940s. He designed elegant public interiors for the Pump Room in the Ambassador East Hotel and the Tavern Club, as well as homes and apartments for Chicago's business and civic leaders. Max Epstein, who was chairman of the board of General American Transportation Company, was a typical client.

Outside Chicago, Marx designed several May Company stores and the Cotillion Room of New York's Pierre Hotel. In addition he designed contemporary furniture and the Pullman Company's first aluminum train car. His sculptural expertise can be seen in Chicago's Lincoln Park, where he designed the Alexander Hamilton Memorial.

Swedish Village House
1487 Tower Road
Winnetka, Illinois

The fairy tale residence at 1487 Tower Road is an anomaly with great visual interest. Curved shingle roofs vie for attention with rough-faced boulder walls. Traditional rectangular windows are juxtaposed with pointed arch and bay windows. Here the irregular is regular, and the visual appeal is unexpected but considerable.

This residence is one of five designed and built by Andrew W. Poulson in 1929. Although similar in scale, materials and detailing, each is a unique and fanciful design. Grouped together on Tower Road they are known locally as the "Swedish Village."

There is no relationship between Swedish architecture as it is known in Illinois and these buildings. Bishop Hill, Illinois, settled by Swedish members of the Janssonist Church movement in 1846, is one of the most significant and best-preserved foreign settlements in the United States. There are no similarities between any building there and these buildings in Winnetka. Rather, the "Swedish Village" is part of the eclectic revival of 1900-1930. It illustrates the resurgence of interest in historic architecture, but with a twist. There is no literal borrowing of Tudor or Classical motifs. The source is the architect's imagination.

Although not in the mainstream, this small development serves as an unusual counterpoint to the North Shore's traditional and modern buildings.

W. F. Temple/Franklin Palma House
Solid Rock
82 Essex Road
Winnetka, Illinois

Despite various early owners, Solid Rock is the name most commonly associated with 82 Essex Road. It was designed in 1911 by Walter Burley Griffin and built of concrete blocks covered with rough cement. The house is a simple straightforward Prairie School design with geometry as its keynote and minimum detailing. There is no applied ornament except for wooden window mullions set in a geometric pattern and I-shaped partitions between the windows.

Solid Rock is unusual because it combines the artistry of two Prairie School architects. It was originally built by Griffin as a flat-roof structure. Its roof was partially covered by an open trellis with large flower boxes at the corners. In 1919, Barry Byrne altered the house, adding steep hipped roofs and a porch at the front. At the same time sculptor Alfonzo Iannelli redecorated the interior. Byrne had met Griffin in 1902 when they worked in Frank Lloyd Wright's Oak Park studio. It was to Byrne that Griffin and his wife, architect Marion Mahoney Griffin, entrusted their practice when they left in 1914 for Australia where Griffin was to design the capital city of Canberra.

Always interested in landscape architecture and community planning, Griffin executed several subdivision designs including one for the nine-acre New Trier neighborhood in Winnetka in 1912-1913. It was to be located just north and west of 82 Essex Road and to contain 30 houses paired around service yards in a pedestrian, naturally-landscaped setting. The plan was never carried out. It was in this neighborhood that the Griffins originally intended to build their own home.

Walter T. Fisher House
949 Fisher Lane
Winnetka, Illinois

Despite its traditional brick exterior, the Fisher House, completed in 1929, is clearly "avant garde" in design, owing a debt to Le Corbusier and the proponents of the International Style. The architect Howard Fisher was owner Walter T. Fisher's brother. Attorney Walter Fisher was a former chairman of the Illinois Commerce Commission.

Fisher created a simple, straightforward house with a plan that accommodated a family of eight. It was to have no reminiscences of any architectural style. Each family member had a private bedroom with angled corner windows to allow plenty of light and air. The basement houses a squash court. Included were several porches and a large roof terrace, a feature typically found in European domestic architecture of the 1920s. The roof is flat. Windows have steel casements. There is no cornice molding, no applied ornament, no historical reference. The look of the house, with planar surfaces and sharp angles, is pure International Style; it is totally contemporary. Although admittedly Fisher assimilated Dutch brick architecture and the work of Frank Lloyd Wright, if the house resembles anything, it would be a ship.

Howard Fisher designed the house in 1927 while a student at Harvard. This was roughly the time International Style was introduced to the United States with Richard Neutra's Lovell House in Los Angeles. But it was five years before European modernism was introduced into American architectural practice by the Museum of Modern Art's exhibition and accompanying book on the International Style.

Fisher went on to make his mark in architecture. In 1932, he founded General Homes, a company that created prefabricated homes. Its concept, which allowed for individualization, was not to create standardized houses; it was to create custom houses using standardized parts.

Crow Island School
1112 Willow Road
Winnetka, Illinois

Child-centered Crow Island School was Carleton W. Washburne's dream. He was superintendent of Winnetka schools and, with the architects, Perkins, Wheeler and Will, made the dream come true.

Every detail of this brick, one-story building was designed to meet the child's needs. Scaled for children, it has front door handles, light switches, bathroom facilities, drinking fountains and blackboards set low. Windows also are low so the children can enjoy the building's park-like setting in Crow Island Woods. Furniture, manufactured by the Depression-era Works Progress Administration (WPA), was moveable and child-sized. Crow Island School's plan was innovative. Three long wings connect to a shared meeting core containing the auditorium, gymnasium, shop, art room, music room and library. Each classroom has an outside door leading to a private courtyard,

workroom for individual projects and bathroom. (Crow Island has 28!) A circular amphitheater is located behind the building.

The school's design is especially impressive because in the late 1930s the typical school was a two-story rectangular box with high-ceilinged rooms, rigid seating and an aloof atmosphere. Warm, child-centered Crow Island School, copied worldwide, totally changed the perception of schools.

When the school was conceived, Perkins, Wheeler and Will was a fledgling firm. Lawrence Perkins approached the more well-known Saarinens, who were family friends, to collaborate. Eliel Saarinen was president of Cranbrook Academy of Art and a widely-respected teacher and architect. His son, Eero Saarinen, who joined his father in 1936, later designed Dulles Airport and the St. Louis Arch. Perkins, Wheeler and Will did the designing, contracting and budgeting for Crow Island School. The Saarinens were consultants and approved all final decisions. Perkins and Will, as the firm came to be known, created an impressive name in school design.

Frederick Newhall House
Breezy Castle
815 Greenleaf Avenue
Glencoe, Illinois

Originally the house at 815 Greenleaf was three stories high with a two-story belvedere tower rising above the front door section. Because of its height, the tower swayed in the wind and, hence, the house became known as Breezy Castle.

Breezy Castle does not fit easily into a convenient stylistic category. Some architectural features are Mansard, or Second Empire, and some are Italianate. Mary Mix Foley, in the "The American House" comments, "The French Second Empire did not long remain a pure style. Americans were reluctant to give up towers and bay windows and rambling verandas which made life so pleasant in favor of Second Empire formality. Many therefore simply built the familiar Italian villa with a newly fashionable mansard roof. This combination of Italianate and Mansardic would become a basic High Victorian type."

Breezy Castle combines a third story mansard roof with Italianate detailing. The convex roof is a full story high punctuated by dormer windows. Italianate details include a cornice with double brackets, bay windows, ornamental hoodmolds and dentil moldings.

It was built in 1871 in Glencoe's beginning years. The Newhalls were early settlers in the village of Glencoe, which incorporated in 1869.

Glencoe was founded by 10 men headed by Alexander Hammond, a retired doctor from Rockford, Illinois. Hammond sought to establish an ideal town with parks, beautiful homes and streets following the land's natural contour. In 1866 he purchased a 520-acre stock farm from Walter Gurnee, former mayor of Chicago and president of the Chicago and Milwaukee Railroad (now the Chicago and North Western). The Glencoe Company was created and land subdivided. Each of the 10 men agreed to build a residence for his family and a second house for sale.

Franklin Newhall cooperated with Dr. Hammond in building his house at 739 Greenleaf and this handsome house at 815 Greenleaf for his brother, Frederick.

Private Residence
341 Lincoln
Glencoe, Illinois

The house at 341 Lincoln is Mansard, or Second Empire, in style and was designed in the early 1870s by William W. Boyington of Highland Park. He is best remembered as the architect of the Chicago Water Tower and Pumping Station, built in 1869.

The Mansard style is typically characterized by a double pitched roof with a steep lower slope. This increases head room in the attic and thus provides an entire floor of useable space. To allow in light, the mansard roof was pierced with dormer windows. Other Mansard style buildings designed by Boyington include the elaborate Grand Pacific Hotel, built in Chicago in 1871, (demolished) and the Benjamin Franklin Allen residence, built in Des Moines in 1869. Today it serves as the Iowa governor's mansion.

The Mansard style originated in France in the 17th Century when architect Francois Mansart executed designs for the Louvre. It later became the distinctive trait of the Second Empire style of architecture, popular in France in the 1860s and 1870s. The Second Empire style derived its name from the reign of Napoleon III (1852-1870), who transformed Paris into a city of monumental buildings that were copied throughout the world. Enlargement of the Louvre during this time helped popularize the mansard roof. In the United States, the Mansard style is occasionally referred to as the General Grant style due to the number of public buildings designed with mansard roofs during his presidency.

341 Lincoln is unusual for a Victorian house; the mansard roof is on the second rather than the third story. Another atypical motif is the large central dormer gracefully set over the front doorway. The roof is also graceful, convex with a concave flare at the bottom.

Alterations occurred in 1919 when two balconies were removed and the front porch was added. This alteration, however, does not detract from the interesting design quality of the structure.

William A. Glasner House
850 Sheridan Road
Glencoe, Illinois

The William A. Glasner house was built as a summer cottage in 1905. Glasner, a bicycle manufacter, sponsored a competition for a servant-free weekend house costing $5,000. Frank Lloyd Wright won the competition and designed this Prairie School house that is built into the side of a ravine. It was completed according to the original plans except for a teahouse, omitted because of budget overruns.

This Glencoe residence was built early in Wright's career when many of his theories of domestic architecture were developing. Wright became the undisputed leader of the Prairie School, the father of a purely indigenous American domestic architectural style that remained popular until World War I when historical styles emphatically returned to the forefront of popularity. His concepts spread to Europe through the 1911 publication of "Early Work by Frank Lloyd Wright," issued in Berlin

by the Ernst Wasmuth firm. The Glasner house was documented in that publication.

This long, low building clearly expresses the horizontal signature of the Prairie School. It has a shallow pitched roof with broad overhangs. Set in stucco, just under the overhangs, is a row of windows containing stained glass in a distinctive tree pattern designed by Wright. Many are "Chicago" windows, a fixed pane of glass flanked by two operable casements.

Other Prairie elements include rough-hewn, creosote-stained woodwork and a Roman brick interior fireplace wall in the living room. White horizontal joints and brick-colored vertical joints give the fireplace wall and chimney a horizontal effect. Characteristic of a Prairie house is the "utility core," which has back-to-back placement of the fireplace and kitchen as the symbolic life-giving element of the house. Rooms and angles of vision surround this core, creating a feeling of spaces extending into the landscape.

Ravine Bluffs Subdivision Sculpture
Sylvan Road
Glencoe, Illinois

In northeast Glencoe situated between two ravines and the Chicago and North Western Railroad right of way is the Ravine Bluffs subdivision. It was designed by Frank Lloyd Wright and commissioned by his lawyer Sherman Booth, Sr. The subdivision includes six Prairie School houses, a bridge and three poured concrete sculptures marking the boundaries. Booth originally lived east of the ravines in a Wright-designed bungalow and had access to a farm which he maintained west of the ravine via a swinging foot bridge. Booth had Wright design a house for him (265 Sylvan Road) and then subdivided the remainder of the farm to build five other houses in that area designed by Wright.

The sculptures marking the subdivision boundaries echo the interplay of geometric elements Wright used in his architecture. Spherical planters are integrated into a rectilinear tower shape that bears the sign "Ravine Bluffs." Some markers contain lights. Each is a strong, simple design statement. The sculptures were probably executed by Alfonzo Iannelli, an early collaborator of Wright on several projects including Midway Gardens (demolished).

The Booth house is the most sophisticated and complex design in Wright's Ravine Bluffs subdivision. Built in 1915, it is one of Wright's last Prairie houses. It departs slightly from Wright's insistent horizontal designs in its three-story height and tower.

The five other houses designed by Wright are flat roofed, moderately priced buildings with plaster surfaces and wood trim. They are based on Wright's 1906 "Fireproof House for $5,000" published in the "Ladies Home Journal."

The bridge on Sylvan Road, the development's northeastern entrance, is a faithfully reconstructed copy of the bridge designed by Frank Lloyd Wright. Built in 1915, it was closed to traffic in 1977 because of deterioration. It was rebuilt and reopened in 1985. The geometry of the bridge replicates that of the sculptures and Booth's house.

J. C. Aspley House
20 Maple Hill Road
Glencoe, Illinois

Built in 1928-1929 for J. C. Aspley, the house at 20 Maple Hill Road was designed by Robert Seyfarth, an eclectic architect of many North Shore residences. In its stonework and low profile, the house is suggestive of a Cotswold cottage.

Robert Seyfarth was born in Blue Island, Illinois in 1878. He attended the Chicago Manual Training School and then worked in George Maher's architectural office from the late 1890s to about 1909.

Around 1909, Seyfarth built his own house at 1498 Sheridan Road in Highland Park and established his office there. At first, he worked in the style of Maher but later designed in the Colonial, English and Continental Provincial styles. While Seyfarth borrowed from historical styles, his creativity gave each house a uniquely Seyfarth quality. His work is more original and eclectic than directly derivative of earlier styles.

From 1925 until 1934, Seyfarth had an office in the Chicago Tribune Tower, then moved his office back to his Highland Park home. Until the 1940s when he hired architect Edward Humrich, Seyfarth did all the drafting and work supervison. He typically used a few craftsmen whose artistry is featured in his designs. At 20 Maple Hill Road, stonemason Caesar Fiocchi probably executed the lannon-stone stonework over the front door.

The Aspley house contains characteristic Seyfarth motifs. The recessed doorway surrounded by ornamental stonework in a symmetrical pattern is a hallmark. Inset dormers are another. There is considerable use of quarried lannon-stone in many Seyfarth houses. Typical of his larger houses is a rambling, asymmetrical plan with a steep roof.

This structure was sited and designed so that almost all the rooms face Lake Michigan. Landscaping was by Gertrude Kuh, a Highland Park resident, who designed landscapes for hundreds of North Shore properties.

E. F. Wieboldt House
Glencoe, Illinois

This elaborate Tudor Revival house was built in 1929 for department store executive E. F. Wieboldt. Architect Ralph Edward Stoetzel's design yields a textbook of Tudor elements that include steeply-pitched, front-facing gables and decorative half-timbering.

The Tudor Revival style was especially fashionable after World War I; only the Colonial Revival matched its popularity. With the widespread use of masonry veneering in the 1920s, the most common Tudor house was faced in brick. The Wieboldt house has a rich tapestry of red brickwork in a variety of patterns. In some areas, the brick follows the lines of the half-timbering; in others it is set diagonally or in a basket weave pattern. Four imposing molded brick chimneys that flare at the top are capped by ornamental clay chimney pots.

Besides detailed brickwork, there is ornamental wood bargeboard with a pendant in the center in the north gable. Rough surfaced lannon-stone set in rectangular blocks adds to the varied texture. This especially rich overall surface texture distinguishes this house from the typical Tudor.

Windows are leaded and heraldic emblems are integrated into some of the panes. The north gable window projects to create a shallow overhang, typically found in Tudor buildings. Entrance to the Wieboldt house is through a porch with slightly pointed Tudor arches, to a front door flanked by leaded sidelights and topped by a leaded transom. A stone emblem over the entrance shows the building date of 1929.

Stoetzel (1892-1970) was educated at the University of Pennsylvania and Columbia University. He began his architectual career at Holabird and Root, then set up his own practice. In 1945 he and his son became partners. Stoetzel lived in Glencoe from 1920 until his death.

Jesse L. Strauss House
110 Maple Hill Road
Glencoe, Illinois

David Adler, called "the last of the great eclectic architects," designed this 1921 house built for businessman Jesse L. Strauss. It is a prime testament to Adler's reputation for designing houses on a baronial scale, usually with extensive landscaped grounds and many secondary structures.

The architect used a versatile approach, designing homes of Italian Renaissance, French Chateau, Georgian, American Colonial and Tudor derivation. Past styles often provided inspiration which he adapted and blended to create works of impeccable quality. Although he undertook commissions on the East and West coasts, most of Adler's designs were for Chicagoans living on the North Shore.

The Strauss house is similar to Adler's home in Libertyville, Illinois. Both contain prominent towers. Adler was inspired by 17th Century French farmhouses that frequently had a "columbier" or pigeon house tower. The Glencoe house's polygonal, pointed-roof tower contains a staircase. Other characteristic French features of the Strauss house include a formal walled courtyard and steeply pitched roofs.

Despite its picturesque massing, the Strauss House design is highly disciplined. Walls are stucco and unadorned. The flared roof is a subtle, but graceful, feature that gives a less static quality to the building.

Adler was born in 1882 in Milwaukee, Wisconsin. He studied at Princeton and the École des Beaux Arts, where he made frequent architectural side trips into the French countryside. On these trips, Adler collected architectural picture postcards, making notations and sketches of details on them.

Returning to the United States, Adler worked a year for Howard Van Doren Shaw, a prominent Chicago "great house" architect. He then opened his own practice and despite limited commissions (approximately 90, including additions), has an unmatched reputation for high quality design.

Alfred Watt House
640 Washington Place
Glencoe, Illinois

640 Washington Place is an example of Georgian architecture embellished with Classical detailing. Built in 1928 for Alfred Watt, the house was designed by architect William H. Furst of Armstrong, Furst and Tilton.

The street side of the house is typically Georgian in the simplicity of design. The other side, on the golf course, is more elaborate with a Classical temple front. Georgian details include rigid symmetry, red brick and multi-paned windows.

Classical features typically found in Georgian architecture include a portico with four Corinthian columns topped by a pediment. Dentil moldings surround the pediment and the cornice of the building. Each dormer set into the slate roof has a broken pediment.

Furst attended the University of Michigan and also was a civil engineer. He designed several North Shore residences and public buildings including North, South and Central Schools in Glencoe, the Glencoe Village Hall and Seabury Western Theological Seminary in Evanston.

Neo-Classical residences built from 1893 to around 1930, such as 640 Washington Place, are easily confused with Greek Revival houses. Both frequently have temple fronts like the stereotypical Southern plantation house. Greek Revival architecture (1830-1860) grew out of archaeological interest in the Greek War of Independence (1821-30) and appealed to liberty-loving Americans who viewed Greece as the birthplace of democracy. Generally these buildings were constructed of wood and were quite literal interpretations of a Greek temple such as the Parthenon. Because the North Shore's period of growth began after the Greek Revival style peaked in popularity, the only examples dating from the 1850s are simplified versions without temple fronts.

Keck & Keck Subdivision House
1201 Terrace Court
Glencoe, Illinois

The house at 1201 Terrace Court is one of 26 in a beautifully landscaped subdivision designed by Keck and Keck in the early 1950s. Developer Harold Friedman of Chicago hired the architectural firm to design this demonstration group of contemporary passive solar houses as moderately priced, low maintenance homes for younger people after World War II. There were five choices of floor plans.

Passive solar features incorporated into the designs include a flat roof that was intended to have a film of water to evaporate and cool the roof and interior. A unique ventilation system consists of a fixed pane of floor-to-ceiling glass flanked by screened, louvered openings set behind doors that open from inside. This configuration allows free flow of air, maximum light and uninterrupted views. Other convenient features include radiant heating in the floors, skylights and floor-to-ceiling built-ins.

George Fred Keck and William Keck attended the University of Illinois. George Fred Keck chose the architectural engineering option rather than the neo-classically oriented architectural school. He opened his office in 1926 and was joined by his brother in 1931.

During their careers, Keck and Keck designed many houses that combined Prairie School and International Style characteristics. This house is Prairie in its use of brick and wood and broad overhangs; it is International Style in its extensive use of glass, smooth surface treatment, flat roof and open floor plan. Houses that reflect both design schools are sometimes called Post Prairie.

In 1979, the Keck and Keck firm was honored at the fourth National Passive Solar Conference: "Keck and Keck was the first architectural office to demonstrate professionally the esthetic potential of passive solar architecture. They were solar pioneers. They synthesized old ideas with new materials in an evolutionary way and created a substantial number of handsome and livable buildings."

Private Residence
Glencoe, Illinois

This house was built in 1956 on a bluff overlooking Lake Michigan. Designed by architect William Ferguson Deknatel, it combines features from Frank Lloyd Wright's Prairie School and European International Style architecture. The result is a style referred to as Post Prairie.

American suburban residential architecture just before and after World War II was largely influenced by Frank Lloyd Wright. This house incorporates such Wrightian features as broad roof overhangs, horizontal bands of clapboard siding and ribbon windows. All emphasize the strict horizontal design.

International Style characteristics are evident in the extensive use of glass and the structure's extreme simplicity. There is no applied ornamentation.

Several subtle visual characteristics make the house unique. At the corners, the glass windows are butt-edged without a vertical wood or metal support, giving the corners a transparent, open quality. The siding on the base is slanted from the ground up to the band of windows. This line is mirrored in the graduated underside slope of the broad roof overhangs.

William Deknatel (1907-1973) was born in Chicago at Jane Addam's Hull House which he actively supported as an adult. He grew up in Chicago, attended Princeton and studied at the École des Beaux Arts in 1929. There he met and married Geraldine Eager, an interior design student. Returning to the United States in 1932, he was among the first students at Frank Lloyd Wright's Taliesin Fellowship for young architects, founded that year.

He returned to Paris in the mid-1930s to study with André Lurcat, an International Style architect. His work became more modern after exposure to European modernism. In 1937, Deknatel returned to Chicago where he established a largely suburban residential practice.

North Shore Congregation Israel
1185 Sheridan Road
Glencoe, Illinois

North Shore Congregation Israel houses the largest and oldest Jewish congregation on the North Shore.

In 1964, on 19 acres overlooking Lake Michigan, the congregation embarked on construction of a sanctuary, school and offices designed by Minoru Yamasaki in collaboration with Friedman, Alschuler and Sincere. Yamasaki's design is representative of a style that co-existed with the modern International Style in the 1950s and 1960s. Yamasaki opposed the more popular, impersonal steel and glass box-like urban architecture. Instead he designed lyrical, romantic and graceful structures with curvilinear lines. He believed architecture should provide serenity and soothe the human spirit.

The large sanctuary consists of eight pairs of reinforced concrete fan vault shells joined at the sides and locked together along the roof's peak. The forms are plant shaped, opening upward like a lily. The roof spaces between the vaults are amber tinted skylights. There are leaded glass strips bordering the walls and arched glass windows at the base that permit a view of trees, lawn and lake. Yamasaki called his design for the temple "architecture of light."

In the late 1970s, need for a smaller, more intimate sanctuary resulted in an addition, completed in 1982, designed by the architectural firm of Hammond, Beeby and Babka, Inc.

The addition is an example of Post-Modern architecture. Typical of Post-Modernism, it pays little regard to the original Yamasaki design. Rather it is a composition of a few strong geometric shapes. The building is a cylinder with punched out square windows ringing the top. Projecting from the cylinder is a large scale porch with a three dimensional Palladian arch.

Thomas Beeby's 1982 addition won several design awards including a 1984 National Honor Award from the American Institute of Architects.

Private Residence
Glencoe, Illinois

Before Stanley Tigerman's name became strongly associated with Post Modernism, he was designing structures that were an extension of Mies van der Rohe's modernism. He describes this phase of his career as "Mies' free plan combined with the free spirit of the 1970s."

Designed in 1975, this house exemplifies the modernist period of Tigerman's career. The roots of the phase lay in client interpretation. Here Tigerman did a masterful job of fulfilling and expressing his client's needs. The 7,500 square foot house features an astronomy dome with a 14-inch telescope, a photographic dark room, a four car garage and an indoor swimming pool. In addition, it has futuristic "high tech" elements as advanced in 1975 as Keck and Keck's House of Tomorrow was in 1933. There is remote control and voice activated lighting. All telephones operate electrical appliances and have digital readouts for temperature and time. It has a remote-controlled robot laundry cart that follows a radio-monitored path.

Although it was an unusual technique for a custom house, Tigerman sought to incorporate prefabrication utilizing off-the-shelf components. The house is built entirely of metal and glass. Glazed aluminum panels take on the changing colors of the sky, lake and landscaping.

Born in Chicago in 1930, Tigerman studied at the Massachusetts Institute of Technology and earned his architecture degree from Yale University. He worked for the Chicago office of Skidmore, Owings and Merrill, and for Keck and Keck, Harry Weese and Paul Rudolph. In 1962 he opened his own office. Currently he serves as Director of the School of Architecture, University of Illinois, Chicago Circle, and is a partner in the firm of Tigerman and McCurry.

Jonas Steers House
120 Belle Avenue
Highland Park, Illinois

When Highland Park was chartered in 1869, Jonas Steers was the first city tax assessor. He also was chief contractor for the Highland Park Building Company.

Among the earliest houses in Highland Park, this handsome Italianate was built by Steers for his family in 1872. It was considerably more unusual than other houses constructed by the company between its incorporation in 1867 and its dissolution, caused by an economic depression, in 1874. The Highland Park Building Company was formed by a group of Chicago businessmen who purchased over 1,200 acres in central Highland Park. Building several Italianate and Victorian Gothic houses on speculation, their intention was to create a gracious community of fine houses.

This well-preserved Victorian boasts wood siding that imitates stone. Similar siding, sometimes called hybrid notched shiplap siding, is found at George Washington's Mount Vernon. Other ornamental details include paired brackets supporting a broad overhanging roof, tall narrow windows surrounded by linear wood trim and an elliptical fanlight over the front door. The vertical window detailing is repeated in the corners of the house.

In 1926 John Van Bergen remodeled the coach house for use as a private residence. Architect James March Goldberg designed a garage in 1979 that reflects the style of the original Victorian house.

Sylvester Millard House
1623 Sylvester Place
Highland Park, Illinois

Surrounded by meadows, wildflowers and woods on the shore of Lake Michigan, this unusual log house was designed in 1893 by William W. Boyington. A path crossing a wooden footbridge over a steep ravine leads to an old gazebo overlooking the lake.

The house offers the peaceful serenity of a hunting lodge or rustic resort, an oasis from the bustle of the city. Its cedar roof blends harmoniously with the massive logs that have rough, raw-edged notched corners and with the rough-faced stone chimneys. The elm logs are from forests near Antioch, Illinois. Today it is surprising to find a log house, such as the Millard residence, that has bark intact through careful replacement.

Boyington was among the first Highland Park mayors and is credited as one of Chicago's earliest architects. Best-known for having designed the Chicago Water Tower, one of few structures to survive the Great 1871 Chicago Fire, Boyington also was architect for Chicago's first Board of Trade Building and numerous hotels and residences.

The Sylvester Millard house, originally built as a summer house, was winterized in 1896. Millard, an attorney, was active in community affairs and instrumental in helping make Highland Park a livable year-round community rather than a summer resort for the wealthy. He addressed such civic issues as bluff erosion. He helped found Exmoor, Highland Park's first country club, designed by Boyington in 1897.

Although several porches have been removed to allow sunlight into the house and a garage has been built underneath, the Millard house retains much of its early integrity. It is listed on the National Register of Historic Places.

The Millards have lived at 1623 Sylvester Place for three generations.

Murray Theatre Lamp Post
Ravinia Park
Highland Park, Illinois

Two intricately ornate Arts and Crafts lamp posts flanking the Murray Theatre entrance are reflective of the cultural achievement associated with Ravinia Park, summer home of the Chicago Symphony Orchestra. The quality of Ravinia's early 20th Century architecture reinforces the experience of a night at Ravinia.

Although Ravinia is one of the oldest summer festivals in the United States, its claim to fame occurred long before the Chicago Symphony Orchestra adopted the park as its summer home in 1936. Designed by Peter Weber, Ravinia Park was originally built by the Chicago and Milwaukee Electric Railroad in 1904 and advertised as "the highest class amusement park in the west." It featured an electric air swing, toboggan slide, casino, theatre and pavilion for classical music. The railroad went into receivership and a small group of North Shore business leaders formed the Ravinia Park Company and bought the park. Its first season, focusing on the production of grand opera with world renowned singers and conductors, was in 1911. Ravinia enjoyed tremendous success until The Depression forced closing of the park for four years. When it reopened in 1936, the Ravinia Festival featured the Chicago Symphony Orchestra.

Entrance gates, the Murray Theatre and remnants of a carousel are the only reminders of Ravinia's rich historical past. The Murray Theatre is a fine Mission style building with Arts and Crafts detailing. Advocating that only objects made by hand with true craftmanship were worthy of the name art, the Arts and Crafts movement started in late 19th Century England as a reaction against the machine-made products of the Industrial Revolution.

Arts and Crafts details in the Murray Theatre include the opalescent glass windows and stenciled ceilings, as well as elaborate wrought iron lamp posts with stained glass lanterns.

Ravinia Park is listed on the National Register of Historic Places.

Ward W. Willits House
1445 Sheridan Road
Highland Park, Illinois

The Ward W. Willits house has been called a great masterpiece of American architecture. It was designed in 1902 by Frank Lloyd Wright and was pivotal in his career development. This house marked the first time Wright had a client with the means that enabled him to create a structure that fully explored and exemplified his ideas. It is the full-blown Prairie house. Its cross-shaped (cruciform) plan with wings radiating from a fireplace core is repeated in residences of every size.

Willits epitomized the American self-made man; with little formal education, he elevated himself from humble beginnings to become chairman of the board of the railway manufacturing firm of Adams and Westlake. He was a perfectionist, knowledgeable in building techniques and meticulous concerning the construction of his house. His committed involvement allowed Wright's creative genius to bloom.

Wright always designed his structures to settle into the landscape. Wherever he was building, his structures were indigenous to their locale. In the Midwest he took his cue from the prairie.

The Willits house epitomizes Prairie School architecture, reflecting the influence of the prairie landscape and translating it into design features. The building is seen as a series of horizontal bands. Broad overhangs shelter ribbons of elegant stained glass windows. These stained glass windows are important to the house because they vary the interior light quality, provide privacy and are the most delicate refined element in Wright's house.

Like all Wright Prairie houses, the Willits house is an exercise in geometry barely related to earlier historical architecture. A mere suggestion of half-timbering serves as vertical counterpoint to the building's incessant horizontal flow.

Listed on the National Register and the Illinois Register, the house is being sensitively restored by the present owner.

Braeside School
150 Pierce Road
Highland Park, Illinois

Braeside School is an unusual educational building because of its Prairie School design. It respects, wraps around and dips into the surrounding landscape. The impression created is that of an inviting home in a beautiful yard rather than a school.

John Van Bergen designed Braeside School in 1928 and added to it in the 1930s. The additions are difficult to discern. Van Bergen undoubtedly was imbued with his neighbor Jens Jensen's philosophy and shared his respect for the natural landscape.

Braeside School has a rough-faced, stratified Wisconsin limestone base. Above is a band of stucco and a row of casement windows. The stone base anchors the building to its surroundings. The windows flood the interior with light and air. Van Bergen was greatly influenced by Frank Lloyd Wright, especially Wright's 1893 William W. Winslow house in River Forest. He worked in Wright's office for many years before moving to Highland Park. Wright's idiom is visible in the intimate relationship of the school to its surrounding landscape. In the front, the long low building with broad overhanging eaves and ribbons of windows embraces the flat front yard. In the rear, the building becomes four stories and dips into the deep wooded ravine. Van Bergen sometimes directly copied Wright, borrowing his signature red square, and his prow window motif. The front entrance of Braeside School echoes the formal symmetry of the Winslow House.

The structure is listed on the National Register of Historic Places.

Rosewood Park Bridge
Julius Rosenwald Property
Highland Park, Illinois

Sheltered in the depths of the ravines, Rosewood Bridge was designed in 1912 by Jens Jensen, one of America's greatest landscape architects. It was built for the Julius Rosenwald family compound; Rosenwald was the president and board chairman of Sears Roebuck.

Reached by a winding pathway, there is a sense of mystery about what might be around the next curve. The path leads from the top of a meadow overlooking Lake Michigan, through a shaded ravine carpeted with trillium, phlox, mayapple, jack-in-the-pulpit, Solomon's seal and other woodland flowers. It is bordered by a low fieldstone wall of horizontal slabs of weathered rock that resemble stone outcroppings. The bridge, built of stratified limestone, originally connected the Rosenwald house to the houses of their two children. Rosenwald's house was demolished in 1936.

The Julius Rosenwald property is now Rosewood Park, located in the section of Highland Park known as Ravinia. In the meadow, the Park District of Highland Park has restored a stone pool with a curved sitting area, a lily garden and a prairie stream that emulates a meandering prairie river. No doubt the rustic beauty of Ravinia, with its deep ravines and natural character, attracted Jensen. It was here that the man, revered as the dean of the Prairie style of landscape architecture, lived and worked, translating his love and respect for nature into art. It was in Ravinia that he designed many estate landscapes, using native plant material and meadows emulating the prairie landscape.

In his private practice, Jensen's client list read like a who's who of Chicago's great fortunes. On the North Shore, the Harold Florsheims, the A. G. Beckers and the E. L. Ryersons all had Jensen-designed properties. Stonework from the Rosenwald estate is among Jensen's finest. The property is listed on the National Register of Historic Places.

Ernest Loeb House and Garden
1425 Waverly Road
Highland Park, Illinois

This Georgian mansion designed by Highland Park resident Arthur Heun is significant not only for its architecture, but also for its setting amid stately oak trees and natural gardens designed by the highly acclaimed landscape architect, Jens Jensen. Only landscape architect Frederick Law Olmsted is more acclaimed in American landscape history. Jensen was a pioneer in the use of native plant material in the Midwest. The elements of nature were, to him, the tools of an artist.

The house was designed in 1930 for Ernest Loeb to assuage Mrs. Loeb's longing for her Birmingham, Alabama ancestry. Like other Colonial Revival houses (Georgian or Federal) it reflects a reawakening of interest in America's early history.

Distinguishing features that place this stately red brick structure in the tradition of Georgian architecture include its red brick exterior, tall hipped roof and Classical symmetry and detailing. The front entrance is topped by a leaded glass fanlight and flanked by sidelights.

Flagstone paths lead to a small-scale Jensen-designed garden, which includes a clearing, free laid stone borders and native plant material. Jensen created a peaceful natural setting, typical of his designs for many North Shore estates. It has been restored by the present owner.

Arthur Heun designed several stately homes for the Loeb family. Although he received no formal training, he attracted a wealthy clientele seeking his traditional Classical style. He also is well-known for designing the country house of J. Ogden Armour.

The Loeb House is listed on the National Register of Historic Places.

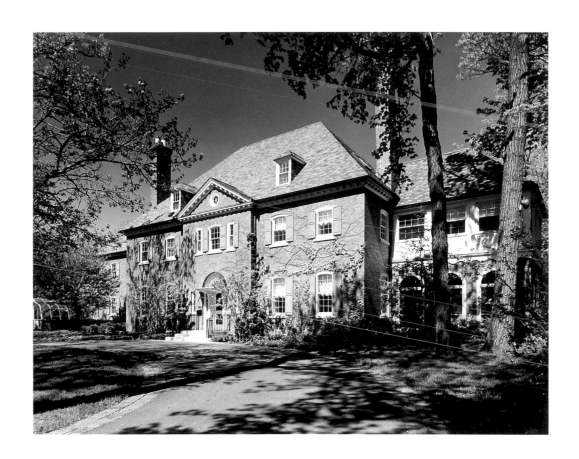

Julius Goldberg House
185 Vine Avenue
Highland Park, Illinois

In 1929, architect Ralph Varney designed this Italian Renaissance house for shoe store magnate, Julius Goldberg, secretary-treasurer of O'Connor & Goldberg Shoes. Goldberg had admired a palazzo in Florence, Italy. He took two architects there to copy the house and returned to Highland Park with Italian columns, marble and a crew of Italian laborers to reproduce the structure.

This two-story brick palazzo is located on two acres. It rests on grounds landscaped in the Mediterranean tradition. The approach is by a circular driveway, surrounding a pond with Ruebenesque statues of nymphs playing musical instruments.

The house is a characteristic Italian Renaissance villa. Typical is the low-pitched hipped roof, covered in varigated tiles. Paired and single full-length arched windows grace the first floor and compliment the arched front doorway with its delicate wrought iron detailing. A two-story corner tower with a conical roof has arched windows separated by twisted columns representing grape vines. Simple gray-blue wooden shuttered casement windows are similar to those found in an Italian dwelling by the sea. Varney executed the design for the villa in brick, a frequently used building material in North Shore architecture. His brickwork shows an appreciation that was probably influenced by his father, head of the Chicago Hydraulic Press Brick Company for over 30 years.

There are few Italian Renaissance Revival houses on the North Shore. It was a style less frequently emulated than Tudor or Colonial architecture during the 1920s when eclecticism was popular.

Private Residence
77 South Deere Park
Highland Park, Illinois

Barry Byrne was a prominent Prairie School architect who specialized in Catholic church and parochial school designs. In 1928 he created the house at 77 South Deere Park, a geometric composition with buff-colored brickwork and no applied ornamentation.

Byrne's Dutch influence is clearly apparent in the crisply articulated ornamental brickwork. His handling of brick is highly creative. He used brick only to emphasize edges that are not square, thereby framing but not adorning his buildings. Bricks interlock, creating textured vertical lines between the doorway and the roofline. The doorway is surrounded by a stepped brickwork pattern that is elegant and distinctly Art Deco in its abstraction and crisp geometry. Triangular motifs are Byrne's trademark. The triangular shape can be found in this house, as well as in his St. Francis Xavier School, 808 Linden Avenue, Wilmette.

Byrne quit school at 14 to work for Montgomery Ward, a job he detested. Exploring Chicago's cultural environment, he visited The Chicago Architectural Club's Exhibition of 1902 where he discovered the magic of Frank Lloyd Wright. He worked for Wright between 1902 and 1908 and later for other prominent Prairie School architects. Wright's lingering influence on Byrne can be seen in the simplicity of design and manipulation of geometric shapes.

Henry Dubin House
441 Cedar Avenue
Highland Park, Illinois

In 1929, Henry Dubin designed this International Style house for his family. Because of The Depression he recognized the need to reconsider housing design and construction techniques. He rejected historical style, designing his own home with geometric, almost cubist massing, flat roofs for sunbathing and ribbon windows wrapping around corners for maximum light and air.

The widely published structure was sometimes called the Battledeck House because of Dubin's technological innovation in the use of steel beams and sheet steel floor construction. He used building techniques more commonly used in naval vessels, hence the name. This shop-fabricated steel construction satisfied Dubin's requirement that his house be fireproof. His ideas were revolutionary and in the January 1932 issue of "Welding," Dubin predicted the day when mass production would revolutionize the construction of houses and commercial buildings.

Born in 1892, Dubin received his architecture degree from the University of Illinois in 1915. He joined the architectural firm of Holabird and Roche before forming his own firm. He studied the work of International Style architect Le Corbusier and others while he was in Europe and borrowed the idiom to meet the needs of his family. Unlike most European International Style houses, which were painted white, the Dubin house was originally left buff-colored. This natural brick fit Ravinia's rural setting.

Soon after the Dubins moved into the house in 1930, they sodded the lawn. Distraught neighbors banded together and approached the Dubins, insisting that sod was totally out of keeping with the landscape character of Ravinia. The Dubins obligingly ripped out all the sod and naturalized the front yard so that it looked much as it does today.

The Dubin House is listed on the National Register of Historic Places.

Ben Rose Auto Museum
370 Beech Street
Highland Park, Illinois

The purest example of Miesian architecture on the North Shore is the Ben Rose Auto Museum. This elegant structure of steel and glass is set on stilts over a heavily wooded ravine. It was designed in 1974 by David Haid to house the owner's antique car collection.

Simplicity and precision are the hallmarks of Mies van der Rohe's architecture. In its simplicity, the Rose structure resembles Crown Hall, 860-880 Lake Shore Drive, or the Farnsworth House, Mies' finest buildings. Like them it is basically a rectangular steel cage. There is no ornament, only I-beams to stiffen the glass and lend a play of light and shade to the building's glass surfaces. It is this structure's fine sense of proportion, not applied trim, that make it beautiful. The steel frame provides a discipline and order that has been compared to the repetition of motifs in Classical architecture.

The interior, like that of the Farnsworth House, is basically generalized space. It is suitable for car exhibition, sleeping, eating or just enjoying the surroundings. From inside the views are spectacular as one absorbs the seasons and is suspended in a natural environment.

It is noteworthy that the whole pavilion was shop fabricated in 17 components and assembled in one day to fit its heavily wooded site. Because of ravine erosion in Highland Park, it is doubtful that construction like this would be permitted today.

Next to the auto museum is the owner's home, a Miesian house designed in 1954 by James Speyer for the Rose family. Speyer was the curator of American Art at the Art Institute of Chicago.

Private Residence
Highland Park, Illinois

According to the owner, "Stanley Tigerman established an environment of air, light, freedom and sensuality when he designed this extraordinary house...in 1985." It is unusual for architecture to evoke such an emotional response, but not when it is Post Modern, the style of the 1980s.

Post Modernism abandons the sameness of Mies Van der Rohe's glass boxes. Purity, simplicity and refinement using basic geometric shapes are replaced by originality and complexity. As Robert Venturi, its early theorist, explains, a Post Modern building explores "richness of meaning rather than clarity of meaning." The style is almost commonplace today, but was shocking in 1979 when architect Philip Johnson designed New York's AT&T Building topped by a huge broken pediment resembling a Chippendale grandfather clock.

Award-winning architect Stanley Tigerman joins Johnson, Venturi, Charles Moore and Helmut Jahn as a pioneer of Post Modernism. Like his fellow architects, Tigerman explores historical styles; he takes a hard look at architecture of the past, but does so with exaggeration, irony and wit.

This Highland Park house exemplifies Tigerman's personal interpretation of Post Modernism. In its Classical symmetry and formal, almost processional appearance, it is reminiscent of an Italian Renaissance villa. The stepped roofline with curves and counter curves is Baroque. But the entrance is toyland. A miniature gabled toy soldier's "sentry house" with double doors is located behind the central porte cochere, inviting guests into the grand entryway.

Sheathed in stucco, the facade has been characterized as a mask by the architect. Behind it, on the interior, are highly polished granite and marble floors and walls, large sun-drenched rooms and a pair of formal staircases leading to the master bedroom. At the back of the house is a swimming pool, flanked by two identical pavilions.

The house, with its complicated design, is full of surprises but disciplined by Tigerman's sense of order.

Private Residence Landscape
Highwood, Illinois

Houses with meticulously landscaped yards along narrow winding streets characterize Highwood, notable because of its long-time tradition of formal landscape design. Examples of carefully trimmed landscapes, like this one with yews pruned into a bridge over the front sidewalk, can be found throughout the town. It represents, in microcosm, the formal Italian tradition of landscaping commonly found in large estates.

Italians, first from Modena, later from Bari and Calabria, settled Highwood in the early 1900s. They found jobs as railroad workers, on construction crews at Fort Sheridan or, with experience paving brick streets in Italy, as street layers. Those with talent for gardening worked on large estates such as Mellody Farm or the Noble Judah property. Major Highwood nursery owners often sent for family members to join the business. Huge Lake Forest estates built between 1900 and 1930 relied on the expertise of skilled immigrant gardeners to maintain as many as 100 landscaped acres, many laid out in the formal Italian Renaissance style with gazebos, pergolas and trellises, often embellished by sculptural fountains, pools, statuary, urns and balustrades.

Formal gardens were the architectural extension of the Classically-designed villa.

Water Tower
Fort Sheridan, Illinois

Fort Sheridan was established in 1887 on wooded bluffs overlooking Lake Michigan, about 25 miles north of Chicago. Construction of permanent buildings began in 1889.

Origins of the fort can be attributed to the decision to build more permanent military garrisons throughout the country and to provide decent housing for soldiers. The Haymarket Riot of 1886 was another major factor leading to the establishment of Fort Sheridan. Significant labor unrest in Chicago prompted a group of wealthy citizens to donate over 600 acres of land to the U. S. government so that a post could be built to protect Chicago's citizens from the rioters.

The private architectural firm of Holabird and Roche (now Holabird and Root) was commissioned to design approximately 66 buildings on the post. Quartermaster General of the Army at the time was Samuel B. Holabird, the architect's father. Using a private firm to design a military installation was unusual and the practice was not allowed to continue.

Originally called Camp Highwood, Fort Sheridan was renamed in 1888 in honor of Lt. General Philip H. Sheridan, a general during the Civil War and Commanding General of the Army from 1883-1888.

This 167-foot water tower, built in 1890 adjacent to the Fort's central parade ground, serves as the focal point of the post. The water tower has a 39-foot base and is flanked on either side by buildings that were originally used as barracks, but now house administrative offices. The tower walls are made of limestone and brick. The roof has been modified from the original steeply-pitched pyramid shape, to a lower-pitched octagonal shape. Still in use, the tower and the adjacent buildings together are approximately 1,000 feet long.

The overall design of the military buildings was kept very simple with little applied ornamentation. Most of the buildings now listed on the National Register of Historic Places, remain intact, providing insight into military life and traditions of 100 years ago.

Post Commander's Residence
Fort Sheridan, Illinois

Buildings in the Fort Sheridan Historic District share numerous characteristics, but the most prominent is use of buff-colored brick, which was manufactured on the post. All original structures are brick with limestone foundations. Except for the water tower, all are less than three stories.

The prime concern of designers Holabird and Roche was to construct buildings for military use; therefore function dictated design. Ornate detailing was mostly limited to decorative brickwork forming arches, friezes, cornices and brackets. Common to the buildings are arched windows and doorways, a motif associated with H. H. Richardson, whose designs were Romanesque in inspiration but greatly simplified.

The Post Commander's residence does not show the expected influence of military functionalism in its design. Rather it is a characteristic Queen Anne design with picturesque features such as corner turrets with domed roofs, projecting roof gables and the typical Victorian front porch. Although originally covered with slate, all roofs have since been replaced. Parapets with terra cotta coping top gable end walls and firewalls.

Most of the fort's buildings have remained in continuous use since they were constructed in 1889 and have had little exterior modification. They have received recognition for excellence of design and historical significance. The area designated as the Fort Sheridan Historic District was listed on the National Register of Historic Places in 1979.

Devillo R. Holt House
The Homestead
570 North Sheridan Road
Lake Forest, Illinois

Known as The Homestead, one of the oldest and most famous houses in Lake Forest was built in 1860 for Devillo R. Holt, a successful Chicagoan in the lumber business. It was originally intended as a summer home, but Mrs. Holt was so impressed with the educational facilities — the Lake Forest Academy for boys and the Ferry Hall School for girls — that a year later the family moved to Lake Forest permanently.

The Holts selected a prime location for their home, high on densely wooded property. The design they chose, a stately Italianate, befits the prominent setting. There have been no exterior alterations so the house is a veritable catalog of Italianate details. Paired brackets separated by attic windows support a broad overhanging cornice. Tall narrow windows are capped by deep segmental hoodmolds; on the side of the house is a projecting bay with tall, narrow, round-headed windows. A front porch with square piers separated by elliptical arches frames the front door. A widow's walk tops the roof. It is not the wood frame building it appears; walls are of brick merely sheathed in wood clapboards.

Holt was a founder of Lake Forest. He signed the letter of incorporation and became one of the city's first trustees. Always civic-minded, he served as a charter member of the Board of Trustees for Lind University (today Lake Forest College) and helped organize the First Presbyterian Church of Lake Forest. The Holt family lived in this house for over 100 years.

Dr. C. F. Quinlan House
334 East Westminster Street
Lake Forest, Illinois

Often referred to as the "Quinlan School" this house was built in 1862 as the first public primary school in Lake Forest. Roxanne Ward Beecher, the first teacher, was the niece of Harriet Beecher Stowe. In 1867, Dr. C. F. Quinlan converted the schoolhouse into a residence. In 1908 the house was moved to its present location from its original site at the corner of Walnut and Washington Roads. Although the porch has been replaced, the house retains much of its original appearance.

This clapboard house has some Italianate features, but is basically a Vernacular cottage. It is a simple, utilitarian structure, restrained in its use of ornament. Italianate characteristics include the gently sloping gable roof with wide eaves supported by large brackets, called modillions, and tall, narrow windows. All windows are double-hung with shouldered lintels. On the second floor, the unusual central front window is Palladian, a tall central arched window flanked by narrow openings with shouldered lintels. Classical features such as this are reminiscent of the preceding Greek Revival style. First floor windows are topped by segmental arches. The entrance doorway has a transom above and sidelights on either side.

Dr. Quinlan moved to Lake Forest in 1859. He became prominent in the community through his participation in the town's development. He was one of the founding fathers of the First Presbyterian Church and one of the 20 trustees for Lind University, now Lake Forest College. He was also the first treasurer of the City of Lake Forest

A dentist, he was the only medical man in Lake Forest until a surgeon arrived after the Civil War. Dr. Quinlan is said to have been one of the first dentists to use sulfuric ether as anesthesia.

First Presbyterian Church
700 North Sheridan Road
Lake Forest, Illinois

The First Presbyterian Church of Lake Forest was completed in 1887. The architect was Charles Sumner Frost, who with his partner Alfred Granger, designed the old Chicago and North Western train station (demolished) in Chicago and many other stations along the railroad's North line. Frost was a Lake Forest resident and elder in the church. Although he was in the office of Henry Ives Cobb when the church was built, he is credited with the design of the church.

The church is Shingle style with its tower and second story wrapped in shingles that gave the style its name. Shingle style buildings, derived from Colonial New England precedents, fit the relaxed suburban image, but there are few on the North Shore. An elegant shingled church such as this is extraordinary.

The spotted stone section of the church is unusual. "Spots" on the stones were formed through the oxidation of marine life metamorphosed into oil. Story has it that the base of the church is of Chicago quarried limestone taken from the Second Presbyterian Church of Chicago, located at Wabash and Washington Streets. The stones, but not the church, survived the Great Chicago Fire of 1871. The church has been renovated several times with well thought-out alterations, the finest being redecoration of the interior sanctuary in 1902, with exquisite windows designed by Tiffany & Co.

In the 1850s, Lake Forest was founded by an association of Chicago Presbyterian Church members who purchased 2,000 acres, setting aside land for Lake Forest Academy, Ferry Hall and Lake Forest College. The First Presbyterian Church of Lake Forest was formed in 1859 with only 14 members.

Durand Art Institute
East Deerpath & North Sheridan Road
Lake Forest, Illinois

Built in 1891 at a cost of $60,000 as a permanent home for The Chicago Art Institute Club of Lake Forest and for Lake Forest College, the Durand Art Institute was named after Henry C. Durand, a leading Lake Forest resident.

The Durand Art Institute was designed in the Richardsonian Romanesque style. Henry Hobson Richardson, a giant of American architecture, so highly personalized the blocky, monumental French Romanesque architecture that the style was given his name. His designs were in sharp contrast to the popular Queen Anne style of the day.

The Durand Art Institute creates a massive fortress-like presence, having been built from large red sandstone blocks from Lake Michigan. A great arched entrance has several richly decorated inner arches, above which are five arched windows set within a steep pediment. At the base of the gable are two finely carved owls associated with Athena, Greek goddess of wisdom. Between the five windows and the entrance arch is a frieze with foliate ornament and the school's name.

In 1976 the building was closed for failure to meet fire code regulations. A 14-month restoration and adaptation for better use by Lake Forest College was completed in 1981.

Architect and Lake Forest resident Henry Ives Cobb was commissioned to design the Durand Art Institute in 1889. Cobb was born in Brookline, Massachusetts (1859-1931) and was one of the first architects formally trained in the United States. He received his degree from Massachusetts Institute of Technology.

Cobb formed a partnership with Charles Frost that lasted from 1881 to 1888. Their more noted Chicago buildings are the Newberry Library, the old Chicago Historical Society Building, the Potter Palmer house (demolished) and several buildings for the World's Columbian Exposition of 1893 and the University of Chicago. In 1902 Cobb moved to New York and established a private practice.

J. Ogden Armour House
Mellody Farm
1500 West Kennedy Road
Lake Forest, Illinois

Jonathan Ogden Armour was the second son of Philip Danforth Armour, founder of the meat-packing company. From 1904-1908, he built Mellody Farm, "A Place Made from Pigs," at a cost of $10 million—$8 million for the house and $2 million for the gardens. Armour bought 1,000 acres of farmland from Patrick Melody, subsequently naming his country estate "Mellody Farm." He added the extra "l" to distinguish the estate from the former owner. When completed, the Armour property was considered one of the grandest estates from the "great house" period.

Although the house is generally eclectic, architect Arthur Heun emphasized features characteristic of an Italian Renaissance villa. Arched loggias, doorways to shallow balconies, red tiled roof and the structure's pastel color are features common to Mediterranean villas.

Mellody Farm's construction was an enormous undertaking. Heun was responsible for dredging swamps, supervising construction of several buildings and overseeing the extensive landscaping. The resulting H-shaped mansion was a 29,000 square-foot, fireproof concrete structure with steel beams for long spans. The driveway was originally 2 miles long and passed through a gate complex with a large courtyard and gatehouse. Armour, on the railroad board, even had a private spur built from the Milwaukee Road Railroad tracks to transport materials for the house. At the price of $65,000, Armour built what was coined "the world's most costly wall" to muffle the sound of the trains. There was a private electric power plant and an elaborate communication system. The estate, in its enormity, contained two lakes, stables, orchard and an orangery.

Today the 200 remaining acres and house are owned by Lake Forest Academy, a coed preparatory school.

Howard Van Doren Shaw House
Ragdale

1260 North Green Bay Road
Lake Forest, Illinois

In 1896 when Green Bay Road was an unpaved horse and buggy route, Howard Van Doren Shaw built Ragdale, his summer cottage, on 50 acres of land. An unpretentious name meaning "uncultivated shabbyness," the house reflects Shaw's love of family, art and attention to detail.

The three-story Arts and Crafts house is stucco with trim painted robin's-egg blue and a slate roof. The front facade has two slightly asymmetrical gables. An inviting center entrance is set under the second story projection to create an open loggia. This recessed porch is supported by unadorned, stout round columns. Along with benches, window boxes and planters, also painted robin's-egg blue, are shutters with exposed wood supports. A simple heart motif, carved into the shutters, is found throughout the house, especially in stained glass interior windows and furniture. Typical of Arts and Crafts, the building's structure is left natural and undisguised. Rafter ends are clearly expressed above the front entrance and roof.

Stressing the love of handcrafted objects and the sanctity of work, the American Arts and Crafts tradition held sophistication and the traditions of Europe in distaste.

Educated at Yale and Massachusetts Institute of Technology, architect Howard Van Doren Shaw worked for two years as a draftsman for William LaBaron Jenney in Chicago. In 1893 he began his own practice which continued until his 1926 death. Shaw received much published praise and was awarded the gold medal of the American Institute of Architects.

An arts patron, Shaw was partial to The Art Institute of Chicago. He served many years as a trustee and helped found the Burnham Library. Today Ragdale, listed on the National Register of Historic Places, stands unchanged as a tribute to Shaw. An artist's retreat, it provides a peaceful sanctuary for writers, scholars, artists and musicians, just as it did for Shaw's family.

Market Square
700 North Western Avenue
Lake Forest, Illinois

Built in 1916, Market Square, an artistically-designed shopping center, was intended by Lake Forest resident and prominent Chicago architect Howard Van Doren Shaw to serve as the town center. Located across from the Lake Forest train station, the buildings of Market Square form a U-shape around a grassy rectangular park. Originally a bank was the focus of the square; today the building is occupied by Marshall Field & Company. The north and south wings contain shops and, unlike modern shopping centers, they retain the character of Shaw's design rather than aggressively proclaiming each store's identity. At the foot of the square is a fountain dedicated to Shaw and including a sculpture by his daughter, Sylvia Shaw Judson.

Market Square reproduces the romanticized vision of an English town market. Its massing, projecting gables with ornamental trim and half-timbering are distinctly Tudor. To these Shaw added arcaded walkways, Italian in derivation, and two towers reminiscent of Austrian country towns. Market Square set the tone for the town center of every village on the North Shore.

Shaw is credited with many elegantly-designed commercial and residential buildings, especially country estates. His clients were Chicago's industrial aristocracy, many of whom lived in Lake Forest. Shaw was without question an establishment architect. His work was eclectic in style — Italian Renaissance, Tudor, and Arts and Crafts. He designed buildings for various purposes including Chicago's Lakeside Press (1897), Fourth Presbyterian Church (1912) and Goodman Theatre (1925).

Market Square, one of Shaw's most innovative designs, is being restored and rehabilitated.

Henry A. Rumsey House

900 East Illinois Road
Lake Forest, Illinois

Henry A. Rumsey, a commodities broker, in 1911 commissioned Shepley, Rutan, and Coolidge of Boston and Chicago to design a house for him on 7½ acres of wooded Lake Forest land. As successors to H. H. Richardson's office, the firm had a well-established reputation. To their credit were the Chicago Public Library and The Art Institute of Chicago. At the request of Mrs. Rumsey, the house was modelled after the Clifford Manor House in Warwickshire, England near Stratford-on-Avon. Coolidge traveled to England to study the manor before designing the Rumsey home.

The house is built of brick with stone trim and a slate hipped roof.

Classical elements incorporated into the building's design include stone quoining, small Doric columns and modillions that support the cornice. It is a large house that is sparsely and elegantly detailed.

Rumsey, like many Lake Forest residents, was an active participant in local government. He served as mayor from 1919-1926. In the late 1920s he was president of the Chicago Board of Trade, thereby overseeing the construction of its new building at the foot of LaSalle Street. After that the tide turned. The Rumseys lost their home during The Depression and moved into Chicago. The house sat vacant until 1941, when the Great Lakes Naval Base used it as officers' quarters until the end of World War II. In 1946, the house became a private residence again. In recent years the house has been renovated and carefully restored.

Clifford Leonard Property
Meadowood Farm
550-75 Hathaway Circle
Lake Forest, Illinois

Early in the 1920s, Clifford Leonard bought 100 acres of farmland in Lake Forest to fulfill a dream. After falling in love with a Normandy Chateau while in Europe, this American owner of a heavy construction company set out to create his own French dairy farm and chateau.

Leonard commissioned Ralph Varney, a well-known estate architect, in 1923 to prepare plans for a residence, an operating dairy and a substantial man-made lake for boating and fishing. Seven buildings were completed: three barns, a chicken house and three cottages for farm superintendents.

The cost of the dairy operations exceeded income, and after only two years it was discontinued. The main chateau was never built. For more than 20 years, the barns and chicken houses were empty, but today they have been all converted into private residences.

The largest structure completed, the cattle barn, was transformed in 1958 by Deerfield architect David Barrow into an 11,000 square-foot luxury home, leaving the exterior virtually intact. French Normandy in style, it is constructed of brick with stone and timber trim. The barn has 18- to 26-inch thick brick walls, copper gutters and spiked steeples. Its round central section is 140 feet high with two wings. There is an adjoining silo connected by a short passageway.

Inside the rounded core of the house the architect designed a sunken living room, dining room, kitchen, den, bath and bedroom with circular stairs leading to a party room, the former hay loft. Opening into the hay loft space is a huge gabled dormer. The north wing is a garage and servants' quarters topped by a dormer and steepled shingled roof. The south wing houses the master suite, with children's bedrooms above. The silo, topped by a tall conical roof, is equipped with an underground bomb shelter.

Albert D. Lasker House
Mill Road Farm
1352 West Estate Lane
Lake Forest, Illinois

David Adler designed this French Provincial chateau for Albert D. Lasker, an advertising tycoon. Built in 1926 at a cost of $3.5 million, the 55-room house was one of 27 buildings on the 480-acre estate. The land has been subdivided and all the original whitewashed brick buildings formerly used as barns and stables have been converted into private residences.

Always meticulous in his eye for detail, Adler was inspired by the elegance of a 17th Century French manor house. Characteristically French are the building's gated formal forecourt and steeply-pitched tile roof. The influence of French architecture, compared to English, is fairly rare and restricted to large, architect-designed houses. There are Cotswold cottages throughout the North Shore but few little chateaus that befit the North Shore lifestyle.

The estate had facilities to meet Lasker's every desire. These included an 18-hole golf course with clubhouse, 50-seat theatre, 12-car garage and a separate building that functioned as a music room and cocktail lounge. All this sat on 250 landscaped acres, including 97 acres of formal gardens and 6 miles of clipped hedges bordering the grounds.

Despite the property's incredible size, the Lasker house and grounds were less palatial than a typical 17th Century chateau; the atmosphere Lasker wanted to portray was to be one of comfort and relaxation for entertaining.

Lasker was a creative and talented man who became a multimillionaire by creating legendary slogans such as "Keep that school girl complexion" and "Reach for a Lucky instead of a sweet."

Noble Judah House

111 West Westminster Street
Lake Forest, Illinois

This estate manor house was built on 40 acres for Noble Brandon Judah, a leading Chicago lawyer. Construction was completed in 1928, taking 4 years to build at a cost of $1.5 million. Modeled after a French-Norman country inn for men of wealth, the 24-room house opens onto a central courtyard. To the west are magnificent sunken formal French gardens.

The architect was Philip Lippincott Goodwin of New York. He graduated from Yale in 1907, studied first at Columbia University, then in France for two years. When he returned to the States, he worked for the prestigious firm of Delano and Aldrich. After 1921 and until his retirement in 1954, he mostly worked alone. He is best known as architect for New York's Museum of Modern Art, which he designed in partnership with Edward Durrell Stone. Coincidentally, he was publishing studies of French architecture as resource material. Goodwin's French design for the Judah house shows the versatility of his interests.

The entrance into the Judah estate is through a half-timbered gatehouse into a cobblestone courtyard. The house is beyond the south end of the court. It has a flared steeply pitched roof that is characteristically French. Projecting pavilions anchor the corners.

Antique architectural elements from historic French homes were incorporated in the interior. The first story oak parquet flooring and living room and dining room paneling came from a 250-year-old French chateau. Elegant French doors and windows with ornate brass hardware extend across the rear of the house.

Judah took time out from his law practice to serve in World War I and was stationed in France, receiving distinguished service medals from the United States and French governments. He served as United States Ambassador to Cuba from 1927 to 1929.

A Camp Meeting Association House
414 Prospect Avenue
Lake Bluff, Illinois

This modest cottage in the heart of Lake Bluff was built in 1885 and typifies the Vernacular style popular around the turn of the century. With whitewashed clapboard siding, a steeply-pitched gable roof and a broad front porch with spindled roof supports, it appears small and ordinary. Its significance is that such cottages are scarce. There are few remaining from at least 50 built between 1878 and 1885 as summer homes for the Lake Bluff Camp Meeting Association (LBCMA). Members of this Methodist group flocked to Lake Bluff during those summers for various religious, social and scenic attractions. Lake Bluff offered a religious retreat in an ideal setting removed from, but accessible to, the city. Lake Bluff developed from a summer place to a year-round village because some of these early vacationers remained.

The LBCMA Annual of 1877 advertised that cottages could "be built within 20 days from the receipt of order for $250." That price included the typical 25-foot lot. The houses were plain — 4 rooms, 2 stories without kitchens or bathrooms. Residents had meal passes for use at several local hotels. The nearest privy was down the street.

The house at 414 Prospect Avenue retains its original facade. Recent owners painstakingly reconstructed the front porch, refinished the front door including hardware and repainted the exterior in the original colors.

This cottage, as well as the other homes on Prospect Avenue, are situated far back from the street. According to an 1878 Lake Bluff survey, the setback allows for a 20-foot easement owned by the village to be used as a bridle path. On Prospect Avenue the lots were approximately 1 to 2 feet above the street so that people could enter their horse-drawn carriages easily at lot level. Such remnants in Lake Bluff are constant reminders of the village's original lifestyle.

Lee Cottage
345 Center Avenue
Lake Bluff, Illinois

A variation of cottages built between 1875 and 1898 for the Lake Bluff Camp Meeting Association (LBCMA), this Stick Style house dates to 1877. Chicago Methodists came to the Lake Bluff camp during summers for religious retreats and country fresh air.

The house is a simplified example of Stick Style architecture in which a building's structural elements are clearly visible. The stickwork on 345 Center Avenue is seen in the open truss under the front gable, the two supporting brackets, the exposed rafters and the wide veranda decorated with simple diagonal braces. The house directly behind it at 346 Prospect Avenue, built for Solomon Thatcher Jr., founder and president of the LBCMA, is another Stick Style example. Few Stick Style houses exist on the North Shore except in Lake Bluff.

Stick Style is a transitional style linking Victorian Gothic with Queen Anne. Its inspiration came from Andrew Jackson Downing whose 1840s and 1850s pattern books of cottage residences voiced the picturesque Gothic ideal. To Downing, the Gothic style embodied "the irregular, spontaneous irrational quality that made the home an emotional refuge from the market place." Given the religious fervor of Downing's philosophy, it is hardly surprising that the houses in these books so closely resemble little churches. This house, with its windows and doors topped by pointed arches, clearly embodies Downing's ideal. Although not many were built, even nationally, Stick Style buildings were often illustrated in later pattern books of the 1860s and 1870s.

Stick Style architecture, probably because of its so called structural honesty, appealed to the settlers of religious colonies. More elaborate examples can be seen in Thousand Islands, New York, and in Oak Bluffs on Martha's Vineyard.

The house at 345 Center Avenue is said to have been built by J. Edward Lee who later became one of Lake Bluff's first trustees. The house has long been known as Lee Cottage.

Otto Kreutzberg House
711 Park Place
Lake Bluff, Illinois

The Italian Renaissance style residence on Park Place was built in 1910 by the Chicago architect Arthur Heun, who also designed the J. Ogden Armour estate, now Lake Forest Academy. It is among his more modest commissions. Italian elements include a cupola and belvedere set above the building's low-pitched roof, broad eaves supported by deep brackets and use of pale-colored stucco.

The Italian Renaissance style was never as popular as other Revival styles, but examples are found throughout the country, built between 1900 and 1930. This style differs from the earlier Italianate style in a very basic way; it is a more literal interpretation of Italian architecture. Architects and clients could easily travel to Europe or had access to photographs so inspiration from pattern books became less an element in designing.

This house was built for Marguerite and Otto Kreutzberg. Marguerite Kreutzberg was a professional artist who had studied in Paris, Los Angeles and at The Art Institute of Chicago. She gained recognition in Lake Bluff by painting a large mural for the East Elementary School in 1926. Although not well-known, her artwork is in New York, Chicago and San Diego museums.

The Kreutzbergs lived on a street known at the time as the "artists' colony" because several artists and literary figures vacationed or lived there.

Elizabeth and Lucy Brennan House
244 North Avenue
Lake Bluff, Illinois

Built in 1917 for two sisters, 244 North Avenue is an unusual Tudor-Prairie style house. The architect, unknown, used English Tudor stylistic elements in half-timbered stucco surfaces and leaded glass windows, but was obviously influenced by the Prairie School architects in his use of deep overhangs and ribbons of tall narrow windows.

Scattered throughout the North Shore are numerous buildings clearly influenced by the architecture of Frank Lloyd Wright and his Prairie School followers. They are not high style buildings, were generally not built for prestigious clients and were usually not designed by architects. Known as "contractor prairies," they illustrate the wide-spread influence of Prairie School architecture. Several can be found in Lake Bluff.

This house was built on three lots for Elizabeth and Lucy Brennan, who were members of The Theosophical Society, "a religious philosophy with mystical concerns" popular in India and America around the turn of the century. Evidence of the Brennan's religious zeal can still be seen on the interior in the design of Hindu gods, goddesses and myths beautifully painted on ceramic tiles surrounding the living room fireplace. It is believed that the unusual number of windows, 121, had some religious significance.

Original facade color and materials, including stucco that had been imported from England, have been maintained. Over the years there have been no exterior alterations or additions.

Lester Armour House

700 Arbor Drive
Lake Bluff, Illinois

The Lester Armour estate is one of only two structures that society architect David Adler designed from 18th Century American Colonial precedents. It is an eclectic mix of Georgian and Federal style architecture. The plan of the house, with outbuildings connected by curving arcades, is derived from Southern plantations. In overall character, the main section of the buff-colored brick is based on the Georgian Hammond-Harwood house in Annapolis, Maryland, designed in 1773 by the great woodcarver-architect William Buckland. Like its Annapolis precedent, the Armour house is a symmetrical brick structure with a projecting central section. Capping both is a bracketed pediment with a central bull's eye window. Adler's elegant Classical entrance with its fanlight also is taken from this Georgian prototype. The interior room shapes and circular staircase are Federal.

Built for Armour in 1931, this house is one of Adler's purest designs. Armour accepted Adler's plans, making no changes whatsoever. Over the years there have been no additions or alterations.

Although this house was designed after Adler was licensed in 1928, at age 44, he had problems getting licensed. Always a designer, not a technician, Adler failed the Illinois exam. After completing 30 houses, he received his license because of several commendation letters from architects and satisfied clients. He never passed the exam.

The house Adler designed for Armour contains at least 28 rooms and 14 bathrooms. With over 5,000 square feet per floor, it is one of his largest estate houses. Originally set on 73 wooded acres high on a bluff overlooking Lake Michigan, the Armour house was designed not for farming but strictly as the family manse.

Lester Armour, born in 1895, was the grandson of Philip D. Armour, the famous meat packer, grain dealer and philanthropist. Armour and Adler were a good match. Because Adler moved in the same social circles as his clients, he understood their needs and capably interpreted them.

Philip D. Armour III House
Tangley Oaks
900 Armour Drive
Lake Bluff, Illinois

Tangley Oaks, like many large North Shore houses, was built on a vast piece of property. Most of these estates have been subdivided. What distinguishes the properties in Lake Forest and parts of Lake Bluff is that the often enormous estates have not generally been divided as intensively or as obviously.

Tangley Oaks is an excellent example of a carefully thought-out subdivision. Surrounded by 10 acres of spreading lawns and magnificent oaks, it rests on a hill overlooking a pond. Its grandeur seems unaffected by the 200 acres of new houses built around it.

Harrie T. Lindeberg designed this English manor house for Philip Danforth Armour in 1932. Lindeberg, born in 1880 to Swedish parents, was educated in the offices of the prominent New York architectural firm of McKim, Mead and White. Although most of his work was for Eastern clients, his Midwestern commissions included several Lake Forest estates and Onwentsia Country Club. Tangley Oaks is considered one of the finest representations of residential Tudor.

Lindeberg's talent lies in his remarkable sense of proportion, his austere reserve in the use of applied ornamentation and his thoughtful adaptation of building to site. Although Tudor characteristics are employed, the architecture of Tangley Oaks is highly disciplined and understated in its elegance.

Built for Armour, his wife and their two children, guests and 26 servants, the 61-room mansion contains 16 bathrooms, each with steam-heated towel warmers. Both the Armours and Lindeberg were enamoured with English Tudor country houses. After studying many such houses abroad, Lindeberg created this mansion with a steeply gabled roof, embellished gutters, leaded windows and tudor arches. The paneling, parquet floors, fireplaces, cornices, furniture and several doors were imported from England. Much of the original building remains.

Since 1954 Tangley Oaks has been the home of The United Educators, Inc.

194

Accomplishing the preservation of historically and architecturally significant structures requires a number of different tools, all of which have been applied on the North Shore of Chicago. The most important ingredient for community preservation is awareness by its inhabitants of their history and the importance of the architecture around them. The preceding pages have contributed to that knowledge. The following appendix discusses the tools available to act upon that knowledge in the interest of preserving the North Shore's architectural treasures.

LANDMARK DESIGNATION

National Register of Historic Places

Numerous structures and sites on the North Shore are listed in the National Register of Historic Places. The Register is a diverse list that includes individual properties or groups of properties. For example, North Shore listings include apartment buildings in Evanston; the Gross Point lighthouse; the Kenilworth Club; the Wildflower and Bird Sanctuary in Mahoney Park, Kenilworth; the Bahai Temple, Wilmette; the Linden "L" Terminal, Wilmette; the Fort Sheridan Historic District; Braeside School, Highland Park; the Highland Park Water Tower; the Lestor Armour House in Lake Bluff; Ravinia Park; and the Lake Forest Historic District.

National Register properties are recognized for their historical, architectural or archaeological significance and are evaluated by a set of criteria. The National Register is maintained by the U.S. Department of the Interior, but Illinois

nominations are coordinated by the Illinois Historic Preservation Agency in Springfield.

As a preservation tool, National Register designation increases community awareness of historic properties and promotes community pride. National Register listing provides for a review process for the effect of federally funded, licensed, or sponsored projects on listed property. It does not restrict the rights of private property owners in the use, development or sale of their listed property. Owners of listed properties are eligible for grants-in-aid when available and, in Illinois, for property tax abatement for rehabilitation of single family, owner-occupied residences. Federal income tax incentives for rehabilitating income-producing properties and disincentives for demolition of such properties have been in effect since 1976.

The National Historic Landmark program identifies sites and buildings of exceptional national significance, unlike the National Register program which includes properties of local, state, or national significance. Potential additions of National Historic Landmarks are surveyed under specific themes in American history, evaluated by a National Park Service advisory board and recommended to the Secretary of the Interior. National Historic Landmarks are automatically listed in the National Register, according them eligibility for tax incentives, grants and protections discussed above. On the North Shore, National Historic Landmarks include the Francis Willard House, 1730 Chicago Avenue, Evanston.

For further information on the National Register, on nominations to the Register, and on various tax consequences, contact the Illinois Historic Preservation Agency,

Division of Preservation Services, Old State Capitol, Springfield, Illinois 62701, Telephone (217) 785-4512. For information on the National Register in other states, call the U.S. Department of the Interior, Telephone (202) 343-9536.

Illinois Register of Historic Places

The Illinois Register of Historic Places lists places that are at least 40 years old and have special historic, architectural, archaeological, cultural or artistic value. North Shore listings include, Frank Lloyd Wright's Ward Willits House in Highland Park. Unlike the National Register, only individual properties, not districts, are listed. The Register is maintained by the Illinois Historic Preservation Agency in Springfield.

Protections for listed properties include review of state funded actions affecting a listed property and, more importantly, review by the Illinois Historic Preservation Agency of any alterations or demolition.

For more information on the Illinois Register, contact the Illinois Historic Preservation Agency, Division of Preservation Services, Old State Capitol, Springfield, Illinois 62701, Telephone (217) 785-4512.

Local Preservation Ordinances

Integral to an effective preservation program is local designation and protection of landmarks and historic districts. This program is created through a historic preservation ordinance such as ones adopted in Evanston, Wilmette, Highland Park and Lake Forest.

Under a preservation ordinance, properties are evaluated for designation according to specific criteria in the ordinance, and, after designation, are subject to review for alterations or demolition. Preservation ordinances provide varying degrees of protection.

Often, as in Evanston, Highland Park and Wilmette, a preservation commission is created with the responsibility of implementing a historic preservation program (See Appendix II for description of the North Shore preservation commissions).

SURVEYS

A survey is used to determine what resources a community has that are worthy of preservation. A local survey is a comprehensive collection of data on the historical and architectural character of a community. The survey is accomplished through field work that includes photographing structures and describing them on site, as well as research in libraries, historical societies and city halls.

The information gathered from the survey serves as the basis for developing public preservation goals. For example properties eligible for nomination to the National Register of Historic Places are identified through a survey. A community preservation plan can be compiled with the data base from the survey, enabling planning and development decisions to be made in a preservation context. A local preservation ordinance designating landmarks and historic districts and protecting designated properties can be enacted, with survey information serving as a basis for property selection. Most importantly, a survey raises community awareness of historic and architectural resources.

On the North Shore, the Glencoe Historical Society is sponsoring a local survey aided by an Illinois Historic Preservation Agency grant. To date, almost 300 properties have been identified for inclusion in the survey. Highland Park and Evanston preservation commissions are conducting on-going surveys.

PRESERVATION PLANS

Once a survey has identified a community's resources worthy of preservation, the community can use this information to plan protection strategies. The local comprehensive planning process can serve as a forum for all concerned interests to consider competing needs of the community. The importance of saving certain buildings may need to be viewed in light of other pressing community issues such as traffic flow, parking, housing needs and business development. In the planning process, interests of all groups can be reconciled.

Preservation plans frequently include a historical overview of the community, description of the community setting, survey of significant resources and notation of properties that might be eligible for local or National Register listing. Also included is an evaluation of the impact of public and private policy such as zoning, building codes, transportation and development plans. Finally, preservation plans include planning goals and objectives and a program for achieving them.

The 1981 Evanston Preservation Plan discusses Evanston's natural and built environment, reviews the accomplishments of the Preservation Commission and identifies long-range goals related to preservation and conservation.

LOCAL PROPERTY TAXES

In Illinois, the Property Tax Assessment Freeze Program provides tax incentives to owner-occupants of certified historic residences who rehabilitate their homes. Through this program the assessed valuation of the historic property is frozen for eight years at the same level as when rehabilitation began. Valuation of the property is returned to market level over a period of four years.

There are specific requirements that must be met to qualify for the property tax assessment freeze. First, the property must be a registered historic structure, either by listing on the National Register of Historic Places or designated by an approved local historic preservation ordinance such as Evanston's or Highland Park's. Second, the property must be used as a single family, owner-occupied residence. Third, at least 25 per cent of the property's market value must be spent on an approved rehabilitation. Last, the rehabilitation of the property must improve the condition of the historic building and include the building's exterior.

The Illinois Historic Preservation Agency operates the Property Tax Assessment Freeze Program. For more information, contact the Illinois Historic Preservation Agency, Division of Preservation Services, Old State Capitol, Springfield, Illinois 62701, Telephone (217) 785-4512.

FEDERAL INCOME TAXES

As of 1976, federal income tax incentives for rehabilitating income-producing properties and disincentives for demolition of such properties have been in effect. These tax consequences have been amended periodically. For current information, contact the Illinois Historic Preservation Agency, Division of Preservation Services, Old State Capitol, Springfield, Illinois 62701, Telephone (217) 785-4512.

EASEMENTS

The easement is an effective preservation technique that has gained increasing recognition. Preservation easements are held by the Landmarks Preservation Council of Illinois on the Henry Demarest Lloyd house in Winnetka and on the Old Rec Center in Lake Forest. Also in Lake Forest, the city holds three preservation easements to control open space around historic structures.

Briefly, an easement is a legal agreement in which certain rights in property are conveyed from one party to another. Easements can be used to ensure the architectural integrity of historic buildings over time by controlling physical changes to facades or whole structures. The use of easements has been encouraged by federal tax laws which, under certain conditions, treat easements as tax deductible charitable contributions.

An easement is typically donated to a municipality or suitable non-profit organization such as the Landmarks Preservation Council of Illinois. The property owner becomes eligible for federal income, gift and estate tax benefits based on the value of the easement as determined by a qualified appraiser. In addition, local property taxes can be reduced to reflect the lowered assessed value of the property. For tax deduction purposes, properties must be listed on the National Register of Historic Places or contribute to a local historic district certified by the Department of the Interior.

For further information on preservation easements, contact the Landmarks Preservation Council of Illinois, 53 W. Jackson, Suite 752, Chicago, Illinois 60604, Telephone (312) 922-1742.

GRANTS

Various types of grants are available to preserve North Shore architecture, but on a limited scale.

At the Federal Level

Historic Preservation Fund monies from the Department of the Interior are funneled through the Illinois Historic Preservation Agency in Springfield. This money is available for local preservation planning and survey activities; some administrative costs, such as preservation commission staff support; and pre-development activity such as architect's plans and specifications and feasibility studies for National Register listed properties. Contact the Illinois Historic Preservation Agency, Division of Preservation Services, Old State Capitol, Springfield, Illinois 62701, Telephone (217) 785-4512.

The National Trust for Historic Preservation, a private non-profit organization, offers consultant service matching grants to help defray costs of consultants such as architects or engineers. Contact the National Trust, 53 W. Jackson, Suite 1135, Chicago, Illinois 60604, Telephone (312) 939-5547.

At the State Level

The Illinois Historic Preservation Agency administers the Illinois Heritage Grants program. These grants are given to local governments or non-profit organizations undertaking the preservation of endangered properties listed on the National Register of Historic Places. The money is available directly for construction costs on a matching basis. Contact the Illinois Historic Preservation Agency.

The Landmarks Preservation Council of Illinois has established an emergency grant and loan fund. LPCI joined with the National Trust in funding a study of preserving the Wilson Estate in Evanston. Contact the Landmarks Preservation Council, 53 W. Jackson, Suite 752, Chicago, Illinois 60604, Telephone (312) 922-1742.

At the Local Level

The Evanston Preservation Commission administers a conservation grant program to aid homeowners in preserving older homes. Grants of up to $2,500 are available to low and moderate income property owners of Evanston landmarks or properties meeting the criteria for landmark designation. Grants are available to help fund restoration of decorative trim, porches, columns and chimneys, painting and reconstruction of wooden siding and removal of artificial siding. Contact the Evanston Preservation Commission, 2100 Ridge Avenue, Evanston, Illinois 60204, Telephone (312) 866-2928.

When seeking information on North Shore architecture, important places to search are local public and college libraries; village or city hall records including building and planning departments and, if applicable, historic preservation commissions; and local historical societies. In addition, there are regional and state organizations, listed at the end of this appendix, which provide valuable information and services.

NORTH SHORE SOURCES

Evanston

Evanston Historical Society
225 Greenwood Street
Evanston, Illinois 60201
Telephone (312) 475-3410

The Society collects and preserves materials and relics of Evanston history. It houses an extensive research library on Evanston history and architecture including a house card file, biographical information, clipping files, city directories and permit files. In addition, the Society is located in and cares for the Charles Gates Dawes House, a National Historic Landmark.

Evanston Preservation Commission
2100 Ridge Avenue
Evanston, Illinois 60204
Telephone (312) 866-2928

Created under a 1975 historic preservation ordinance, the Evanston Preservation Commission is an 11-member city commission that includes among its duties the study and recommendation of structures to become Evanston landmarks. Information on the more than 780 Evanston landmarks, as well as planning and preservation materials, is available from the commission. In addition to review and protection of designated landmarks, the commission conducts public education programs, provides technical assistance and, in some instances, financial aid to landmark owners.

Preservation League of Evanston
P.O. Box 5347
Evanston, Illinois 60204

The Preservation League is a non-profit community organization that seeks to educate about Evanston's architectural character. The League publishes a newsletter, offers a resource center on restoration techniques and tradesmen referrals, provides speakers on preservation subjects and sponsors trips to areas of architectural and historical interest.

Wilmette

Wilmette Preservation Commission
Wilmette Historical Board and Museum
565 Hunter Road
Wilmette, Illinois 60091
Telephone (312) 256-5838

The Historical Museum contains historical artifacts and archives pertaining to Wilmette history. In the collection are numerous resources for researching Wilmette architecture such as abstracts of titles; books on architectural styles, house walk programs, real estate listings, an owner's index, street directories, telephone books, building permit receipts, house files by street address, information on noted architects in Wilmette and data on houses recognized by the Wilmette Historical Society as having historical and architectural merit.

Wilmette Preservation Commission
Wilmette Preservation Board
1200 Wilmette Avenue
Wilmette, Illinois 60091
Telephone (312) 251-2700

Created in 1988, the Wilmette Preservation Commission's purposes are to create public awareness in the importance of preserving landmarks, to provide information on maintenance of landmarks, to recommend to the Village Board the designation of landmarks and to review alterations and demolitions of designated landmarks.

Kenilworth

Kenilworth Historical Society
415 Kenilworth Avenue
P. O. Box 81
Kenilworth, Illinois 60043
Telephone (312) 251-2565

The Kenilworth Historical Society contains extensive information on the history and architecture of Kenilworth. There are numerous photographs of structures and a house card file with information on architects and previous owners. Additionally, there is a research library and museum with changing exhibits on Kenilworth history.

Winnetka

Winnetka Historical Museum
1140 Elm Street (museum location)
510 Green Bay Road (mailing address)
Winnetka, Illinois 60093
Telephone (312) 446-7736

The Winnetka Historical Museum is a joint project between the Village of Winnetka and the Winnetka Historical Society. The museum contains a research library, costume collection, photographs and information on Winnetka's "Heritage Homes" program, those homes of historical significance that are more than 75 years old.

Glencoe

Glencoe Historical Society
305 Randolph (museum location)
999 Green Bay Road (mailing address)
Glencoe, Illinois 60022

The Glencoe Historical Society has a museum of local history and archives containing photographs, clippings, letters, papers, memorabilia, real estate listings and costumes. There also are files from the historical and architectural survey conducted in part with an Illinois Historic Preservation Agency grant. The survey identifies almost 300 structures of historical and architectural importance and contains photographs and information on owners, alterations, building dates and architects.

Highland Park

Highland Park Historical Society
P.O. Box 56
326 Central Avenue
Highland Park, Illinois 60035
Telephone (312) 432-7090

The Highland Park Historical Society contains local memorabilia, a reference library, photographs and a room devoted to the history of Ravinia Park.

Highland Park Preservation Commission
City Hall
1707 St. Johns Avenue
Highland Park, Illinois 60035
Telephone (312) 432-0800

The Highland Park Preservation Commission is a 9-member city commission that administers the city's historic preservation program. The commission maintains information on Highland Park landmarks and historic districts. Its major function is identification and designation of landmarks and their protection from adverse changes. The commission provides public education on Highland Park history and architecture and provides advice on maintenance and restoration problems. As of 1988, there were 38 landmarks designated.

Fort Sheridan

Fort Sheridan Museum
Building 33
Fort Sheridan, Illinois 60037-5000
Telephone (312) 926-2173/2309

The Fort Sheridan Museum is housed in the 1890 guard house, one of the first buildings completed at Fort Sheridan. Information is available on the architecture of the Fort Sheridan National Register Historic District.

Lake Forest/Lake Bluff

Lake Forest Foundation for
   Historic Preservation
Box 813
Lake Forest, Illinois 60045

The Foundation is a community organization that encourages the preservation of Lake Forest's historic visual character. Among its activities, the Foundation has funded a survey of Lake Forest architecture, as well as various studies and the photography of significant

buildings and neighborhoods. The Foundation spearheaded the renovation of the Lake Forest train station and of other historic buildings. It publishes a news-letter and sponsors workshops on preservation of Lake Forest.

Lake Forest/Lake Bluff Historical Society
P.O. Box 82
Lake Forest, Illinois 60045
Telephone (312) 234-5253

The historical society collects and preserves documents, records, photographs and other objects related to the history of Lake Forest and Lake Bluff. Included in the collection is a file on Lake Forest homes.

Department of Planning and Development
City of Lake Forest
200 East Deerpath
Lake Forest, Illinois 60045
Telephone (312) 234-2600

The department maintains survey maps and information on the Lake Forest Residential Historic Preservation District, a zoning district created for its unique character. Review for special use permits, demolition of structures and subdivisions of land is required in the district.

Elmer Vliet Historical Center
121 East Sheridan Road
Lake Bluff, Illinois 60044
Telephone (312) 234-9405/9407

Located in the original East School built in 1895, the center provides students and the community an opportunity to appreciate their local heritage. Included in the displays are photographs, documents, costumes and other memorabilia relating to Lake Bluff history.

OTHER SOURCES OF INFORMATION

David Adler Cultural Center
1700 North Milwaukee Avenue
Libertyville, Illinois 60048
Telephone (312) 367-0707

Housed in David Adler's former summer home, the center's resources include biographical information on Adler, photographs of Adler's houses, a list of addresses of Adler's work.

Lake County Museum
Lakewood Forest Preserve
Rte 176 and Fairfield Road
Wauconda, Illinois 60084
Telephone (312) 526-7878

The Lake County Museum contains a non-circulating reference library open by appointment, which includes photographs and books on Lake County history. The museum houses the Curt Teich Postcard Collection.

Waukegan Historical Society
17 North Sheridan Road
Waukegan, Illinois 60085
Telephone (312) 336-1859

The society's collection includes county directories prior to 1920 and biographies of Lake County individuals.

Northbrook Public Library
1201 Cedar Lane
Northbrook, Illinois 60062
Telephone (312) 272-6224

This library contains the most comprehensive collection in the North Suburban Library System of books on architecture, architectural history, landscape architecture and city planning.

Ryerson and Burnham Library of
    Architecture, Art Institute of Chicago
South Michigan Avenue
Chicago, Illlinois 60603
Telephone (312) 443-3666

The Ryerson and Burnham Library has the most extensive collection in the Chicago area on architecture. Included are the "Burnham" and "Avery" indexes which include listings of sources for articles on North Shore buildings from old architectural journals. Also available is biographical information on architects, architects' drawings and archival collections of significant Midwest architects. Art Institute membership is a prerequisite for use of the library.

Chicago Historical Society
North Clark and West North Avenue
Chicago, Illinois 60614
Telephone (312) 642-4600

The Chicago Historical Society contains old directories, blue books, histories, old photographs and some original plans. While the majority of information pertains to Chicago, there is information on architects who practiced on the North Shore and on North Shore residents.

Landmarks Preservation Council of Illinois
53 West Jackson, Suite 752
Chicago, Illinois 60604
Telephone (312) 922-1742

LPCI is a statewide membership organization that promotes the preservation of Illinois architecture. LPCI maintains a reference library on preservation for members' use and provides members with technical information and assistance. LPCI actively promotes preservation on the North Shore.

The National Trust for Historic Preservation
Midwest Regional Office
53 West Jackson, Suite 1135
Chicago, Illinois 60604
Telephone (312) 939-5547

The National Trust is a national membership organization that promotes preservation of historically and architecturally significant structures. The Trust's Midwest office is an information source on aspects of preservation, including preservation tools, discussed in Appendix I, technical preservation assistance and small consultant service grants. It is open by appointment.

Illinois Historic Preservation
    Agency (II IPA)
Old State Capitol
Springfield, Illinois 62701
Telephone (312) 782-4836

The IHPA is the state agency responsible for collecting, preserving and interpreting the history of Illinois. As a source of information on North Shore architecture, the IHPA is the repository of documentation on sites listed in the National Register of Historic Places (Appendix I). It also maintains a reference card file, by architect, of Illinois buildings that were photographed in old architectural journals.

200

Arpee, Edward. *Lake Forest, Illinois, History and Reminiscences, 1861-1961*. Lake Forest: Lake Forest Rotary Club, 1964.

Bach, Ira J. *A Guide to Chicago's Historic Suburbs on Wheels and on Foot*. Chicago: Swallow Press, Ohio University Press, 1981.

Baird and Warner. *A Portfolio of Fine Apartment Homes*. Chicago: Baird and Warner, 1928.

Blake, Joseph. *Glossary*. Privately distributed by the Evanston Preservation Commission. Evanston, Illinois.

Bennett, Edward H. *Plan of Winnetka*. 1921

Berger, Philip, ed. *Highland Park, American Suburb at its Best*. Highland Park: The Highland Park Landmark Preservation Committee, 1984.

Blumenson, John J. G. *Identifying American Architecture: A Pictorial Guide to Style and Terms, 1600-1945*. Nashville: American Association for State and Local History, 1977.

Brooks, H. Allen. *The Prairie School: Frank Lloyd Wright and His Midwest Contemporaries*. Toronto and Buffalo: University of Toronto Press, 1972.

Bushnell, George D. *Wilmette: A History*. Wilmette: The Wilmette Bicentennial Commission, 1980.

Carbol, Betty Williams. *The Making of a Special Place: A History of Crow Island School, Winnetka, Illinois*. Privately Published.

Chicago Architects Design: A Century of Architectural Drawings from the Art Institute of Chicago. New York: The Art Institute of Chicago and Rizzoli International Publications, Inc., 1982.

Cohen, Stuart E. *Chicago Architects*. Chicago: Swallow Press, 1976.

Condit, Carl W. *Chicago, 1910-29: Building, Planning, and Urban Technology*. Chicago and London: University of Chicago Press, 1974.

Dickinson, Lora Townsend. *The Story of Winnetka*. Winnetka: Winnetka Historical Society, 1956.

Downing, Andrew Jackson. *Cottage Residences*. (Orig. Ed. 1842, Reprinted 1873 under the title *Victorian Cottage Residences*). New York: Dover Publications, 1981.

Ebner, Michael H. *Creating Chicago's North Shore*. Chicago: The University of Chicago Press, 1988.

Eaton, Leonard K. *Landscape Artist in America: The Life and Work of Jens Jensen*. Chicago: The University of Chicago Press, 1964.

——————. *Two Chicago Architects and Their Clients: Frank Lloyd Wright and Howard Van Doren Shaw*. Cambridge: MIT Press, 1969.

Fishman, Robert. *Bourgeois Utopias: The Rise and Fall of Suburbia*. New York: Basic Books, Inc., 1987.

Gebhard, David and Deborah Nevis. *200 Years of American Architectural Drawing*. New York: Whitney Library of Design, 1977.

Grow, Lawrence. *On the 8:02: An Informal History of Community by Rail in America*. New York: Mayflower Books, Inc., 1979.

Harris, Cyril. *Dictionary of Architecture and Construction.* New York: McGraw-Hill Boon Company, 1975.

Harnsberger, Caroline Thomas. *Winnetka: The Biography of a Village.* Evanston: The Schori Press, 1977.

Hitchcock, Henry Russell and Philip Johnson. *The International Style: Architecture Since 1922.* New York: Da Capo Press, 1973.

Kenilworth, the First Fifty Years. Kenilworth: Village of Kenilworth, 1947.

Maass, John. *The Gingerbread Age: A View of Victorian America.* New York: Bramhall House, 1967.

Marquis, Alfred Nelson. *Who's Who in Chicago: The Book of Chicagoans.* Chicago: A.N. Marquis & Co., 1905, 1911, 1917, 1931, 1936.

McAllister, Virginia and Lee. *A Field Guide to American Houses.* New York: Alfred A. Knopf, 1985.

Peisch, Mark L. *The Chicago School of Architecture.* New York: Random House, 1964.

Perkins, Margery Blair. *Evanstoniana: An Informal History of Evanston and its Architecture.* Ed. Barbara J. Buchbinder-Green. Evanston and Chicago: Evanston Historical Society and Chicago Review Press, 1985.

Poppeliers, John C., S. Allen Chambers, Jr., Nancy B. Schwartz. *What Style Is It? A Guide to American Architecture.* Washington, D.C.: The Preservation Press, National Trust for Historic Preservation, 1983.

Pratt, Richard. *David Adler: The Architect and His Work.* New York: M. Evans and Company, 1970.

Randall, Frank A. *History of the Development of Building Construction.* Urbana: The University of Illinois Press, 1949.

Scully, Vincent J., Jr. *The Shingle Style: Architectural Theory and Design from Downing to the Origins of Wright.* New Haven: Yale University Press, 1971.

Storer, William A. *The Architecture of Frank Lloyd Wright: A Complete Catalog.* Cambridge: MIT Press, 1973.

Thulin, Marjorie, ed. *Glencoe: Lights and 100 Candles, 1869-1969.* Glencoe: Glencoe Historical Society, 1969.

Vliet, Elmer. *Lake Bluff, The First Hundred Years.* Chicago: R.R. Donnelley Sons & Co., 1985.

Whiffen, Marcus. *American Architecture Since 1780: A Guide to the Styles.* Cambridge: MIT Press, 1969.

Withey, Henry F. and Elsie Rathburn Withey. *Biographical Dictionary of American Architects (Deceased).* Los Angeles: Hennessey & Ingales, 1970.

Wittelle, Marvyn. *Pioneer to Commuter. The Story of Highland Park.* Highland Park: Rotary Club of Highland Park, 1958.

_____. *28 Miles North: The Story of Highwood.* Highwood: The Highwood History Foundation, Inc., 1953.

Zukowsky, John, ed. *Chicago Architecture 1872-1922.* Chicago and Munich: The Art Institute of Chicago and Prestel-Verlag, 1987.

General Architectural Terms—originally printed and distributed as "This Gingerbread is Not for Eating," by The Junior League of Evanston, Inc., 1987.

Arch—A structure of stones, bricks, or other materials supporting each other by mutual pressure to span an opening. Different types of arches include Romanesque, Gothic and Tudor.

Ashlar—Squared stone block construction for building or facing a wall.

Balustrade—An entire railing system including a top rail and its vertical supports or balusters.

Banded or Ribbon Windows—A series of windows separated by mullions.

Belvedere—A structure designed to command a view.

Bargeboard—A board, often carved, attached to the edge of a gable roof, as a decorative trim. Also called vergeboard, "gingerbread."

Bay Window—A triple window that projects from an exterior wall. Commonly rises more than one story from the ground.

Board and Batten—Vertical siding made from wide boards; the spaces between the boards are covered by narrow, overlapping, wooden strips.

Bracket—A support under eaves or other overhangs, often more decorative than functional.

Cantilever—A horizontal projection extending from the wall of a building without visible means of support.

Capital—The decorated top part of a column or pilaster. Classical Greek orders of architecture can be identified by their distinctive Doric, Ionic or Corinthian capitals.

Cartouche—A curved scoll-like panel often inscribed or decorated, set on the exterior wall of a building.

Casement Window—A hinged window that opens outward.

Chicago Window—A triple window, with matching side windows that open, flanking a wider, fixed central pane.

Chimney Pot—Extension of the flue above the chimney. Usually decorated.

Clapboard—Wide overlapping boards laid horizontally on the exterior surfaces of frame buildings.

Colonnade—A row of columns.

Coping—A protective cap on the top of a wall or parapet.

Cresting—A light metal ornament carried along the top of the roof.

Cupola—A small domed structure at the top of a building.

Dentil Moldings—Square or rectangular blocks, alternating with blank spaces, give this molding the appearance of a row of teeth. Most frequently used on an exterior cornice under the eaves.

Dormer Window—A window set vertically into a sloping roof.

Eave—A projecting roof overhang, a cornice.

Eclectic—As an architectural term, this applies to buildings incorporating a variety of features from different styles.

Entablature—In classical architecture, the ornamental beam member carried by the columns resting on the capitals. It consists of the architrave, frieze and cornice.

Facade—The exterior face of a building.

Fanlight—A semi-circular window, resembling an open fan, often set over a window or door.

Finial—An ornament that forms the pointed top of a pinnacle or spire.

Frieze—An ornamental band along the top of a wall.

Gable—The triangular portion of the end of a building between the two slopes of a pitched roof.

Gabled Roof—The gabled roof has two planes meeting in the center with a triangular end wall.

Gambrel Roof—There are two slopes on each side of a gambrel roof, meeting in a central ridge; the lower slope having a steeper pitch.

Gingerbread—Heavily carved, ornamental bargeboards.

Half-Timbered—A heavy timber frame with the wide spaces between the timbers filled with plaster or brick.

Hipped Roof—A roof that slopes in four directions from a central ridge.

Hood-Molding—Projecting arch molding over a door or window.

Jamb—The framing sidepiece or post of a door or window.

Key Stone—The center stone in an arch.

Leaded Glass—Small panes of clear or stained glass, held in place by lead strips.

Lintel—A horizontal wood beam or stone slab, over a door or window opening.

Loggia—A covered arcade, open on one or more sides, supported by a row of columns.

Mansard Roof—A dual pitched roof that slopes in four directions from a central ridge or point. It encloses an entire floor of living space.

Masonry—The use of stone or brick in construction.

Massing—The overall shape of the building.

Modillion—A large horizontal bracket supporting a roof cornice.

Molding—Contoured long wood strips used to finish or decorate a wall, door or window.

Mullion—A vertical separation between panes of glass.

Muntin—A secondary framing member bar that supports and separates panes of window glass.

Oriel Window—A projecting bay window that does not touch the ground.

Palladian Window—A triple window, with matching rectangular side windows, and a wider arched central window.

Parapet—That part of the wall that extends beyond the roof of a building.

Pediment—A shallow triangular structure found over a door, window or niche resembling a classical temple front. Variations include a curved and broken pediment.

Pillar—A slender supporting column.

Pilaster—A flattened semicircular or squared column attached to the wall. Often has capital and base.

Porte-Cochere—A covered entrance porch, large enough to admit vehicles.

Portico—An open porch, covered by a roof, supported by classical columns.

Quoins—Right-angled stones or sets of bricks, raised to accentuate the exterior corners of a building.

Rail—A horizontal bar between individual window panes.

Sash—The framework of a window, may be movable or fixed.

Segmental Arch—A portion of an arch that is less than a semi-circle.

Shingles—Overlapping pieces of wood or asphalt covering the roof or walls of a house.

Sullivanesque—Foliate ornament in the style of Chicago School architect Louis Sullivan.

Terra Cotta—Hard glazed or unglazed fired clay, molded to form building ornament. Usually larger in size than a brick.

Transom—Window at the top of a door. Sometimes called a transom window.

Turret—A small tower, not touching the ground, rising above the main floors of a building.

Veranda—A roofed open porch on a terrace along the front or side of a building.

Junior League of Evanston

Karen Arterburn
Beth Bernardi
Belinda Blanchard
Kathleen Cassidy
Kirby Colson
Nancy Dorr
Diane Drinker
Susan Duncan
Celia Duroe
Judy Dutterer

Anita Eller
Dolores Eyler
Jan Gargula
Barbara Griffin
Chris Hagan
Molly Heald
Kathy Hurley
Muggsy Jacoby
Mary Johnson
Paula Killian
Claudia Lane

Judy Lowman
Sue Marineau
Sharon McGee
Beth Mikel
Pat Nemrava
Cathie Ottmar
Ellen Paseltiner
Sandy Plochman
Sandy Rau
Deborah Reed
Betsy Ryberg

Carol Smith
Ann Spieth
Ann Springborn
Suzanne Thomas
Katie Vail
Pat Valko
Cathy Weaver
Bonnie Winn
Julie Withers
Caren Wolf

Community

Nick Anderson
Boyd Anderson
Leah Axelrod
Evie Barriger
Joe Blake
Robert E. Blanchard
Tom Breuer
Alyson Breuer
C. William Brubaker
Marianne Crosby
George Cyrus
Onnie Darrow
Robert C. Davis

Daria Durham
Trish Early
Holly Fiala
Steve Fiori
Walter Fisher
Cindy Fuller
William Furst
Mrs. Walter A. Gatzert
Richard W. Gilbert
Alice Glicksburg
Adam Goldman
Virginia Grimm
Gail Hodges

Eddie Furst Howell
Carolyn Johnson
Herman H. Lackner
John Mariani
Mary McWilliams
Everett Millard
JoAnn Nathan
Rosella O'Reilly
Seymour Persky
Bob Piper
Eileen Ramm
Marian Roberts
Ellen Shubart

Julia Sniderman
Walter Sobel
Roy Solfisburg
Gwen Sommers Yant
Ethel Spindell
Ann Swallow
Stanley Tigerman
Barbara Welsch
Max Whitman
Mary Woolover
Carol Wyant
Joe Zendell

Organizations & Companies

Evanston Historical Society
Evanston Preservation Commission
Glencoe Historical Society
Highland Park Historical Society
Highland Park Historic Preservation
   Commission
Illinois Arts Council
Illinois Historical Preservation Agency
   (formerly Department of Conservation)
Kenilworth Historical Society
Landmark Preservation Council of Illinois

Lake Bluff/Lake Forest Historical Society
Lake Forest Academy
Historical Society of Lake County
National Trust for Historic Preservation
Pioneer Press, Inc.
Stone Container Corporation
Strategic Management
Stuart James Foundation
Wilmette Historical Society
Winnetka Historical Society

Any omission is accidental and with sincere apology.